BRAND MANAGEMENT 101

101 ✓ LESSONS FROM
REAL-WORLD
MARKETING

BRAND MANAGEMENT 101

MAINAK DHAR

101 LESSONS FROM REAL-WORLD MARKETING

BICENTENNIAL
1807
WILEY
2007
BICENTENNIAL

John Wiley & Sons (Asia) Pte., Ltd.

This publication is designed to provide accurate and authoritative information in regard to the subject matter covered. It is sold with the understanding that the publisher is not engaged in rendering professional services. If professional advice or other expert assistance is required, the services of a competent professional person should be sought.

Other Wiley Editorial Offices

John Wiley & Sons, 111 River Street, Hoboken, NJ 07030, USA
John Wiley & Sons, The Atrium Southern Gate, Chichester PO19 8SQ, England
John Wiley & Sons (Canada) Ltd, 5353 Dundas Street West, Suite 400, Toronto Ontario M9B 6HB. Canada
John Wiley & Sons Australia Ltd. 42 McDougall Street, Milton, Queensland 4064, Australia
Wiley-VCH, Bosch Strasse 12, D-69469 Weinheim, Germany

Library of Congress Cataloging-in-Publication Data

ISBN 978-0-470-82229-6

Wiley Bicentennial Logo: Richard J. Pacifico
Typeset in 10/13.5 Points ITC Novarese by JC Ruxpin Pte Ltd
Printed in Singapore by Saik Wah Press Pte Ltd
10 9 8 7 6 5 4 3 2 1

TABLE OF CONTENTS

Never tell anyone that you're writing a book, going on a diet, exercising, taking a course, or quitting smoking. They'll encourage you to death.

- Lynn Johnston

Now having successfully tried all of the above, I must say I disagree with the quote, especially when it comes to writing a book. When you're trying hard to get down to writing at night after a tiring day at the office, or waiting for the dreaded rejection slip that hangs over every writer's head like a guillotine, you need all the encouragement you can get. However, if there's anyone who needs even more encouragement, it must be the aspiring writer's spouse, who has to accept mood swings, ideas coming into one's head in mid conversation, and the unenviable task of reading the drafts, all are occupational hazards.

So first and foremost, if there's one person who is at the very core of anything I end up achieving as a writer and as a person, it's my wife Puja. As always, I'm sitting right next to her as I write these lines, and wondering what I must have done so right in some previous life to be lucky enough to be with her in this one. Thanks for everything, sweetheart.

Fluffy will never get around to reading this, but here's a tip for aspiring writers—get a Shih Tzu puppy. Playing with her may be the best cure ever for writer's block.

Huge thanks also to C.J. Hwu, Joel Balbin, Cynthia Mak, Louise Koh and the team at John Wiley & Sons for helping bring this book to life.

INTRODUCTION

Before trying to impress you with reasons why you should read this book, let me give you a few reasons why you should not read it. First, I am no highbrow academic and I do not have a PhD in marketing. In fact, I was so glad that I would not have to write any more exams for the rest of my life that I left a fair bit of my last paper in business school unfinished. Second, you probably will not learn a lot of new theoretical constructs and models in this book—there are some really great books out there on the subject, written by people better qualified to write them than me, so I won't waste my time and yours trying.

Still With Me? Great.

Before I talk any more about marketing, let me tell you a story. Many years ago, when I was still in school, I developed a fascination for martial arts. I started reading books that all promised to teach self defense. Many of them were written by supposed experts, and most made it look all too easy, with their step-by-step instructions and nicely drawn diagrams. Soon I was practicing the steps at home, and had started on the breathing and physical exercises some of the books laid out. A few months later, I joined karate classes at a YMCA near my home, starting an association that was to last nearly seven years of scarred knuckles and aching ribs.

When I started the classes, I felt pretty good about all that I had learned, and when my *sensei* started teaching theory to the class, I thought I already knew it all. And then I had my first sparring bout with a large, brooding boy who stood a few inches taller than me and had been learning karate for over a year. All the theory I had learned, all the practice I had done at home, all the things I thought I knew about karate dissipated in one single moment.

That was when I tasted my own blood.

I was frozen like a deer in the headlights. It was just a glancing blow that had cut my lip, but the shock of being hit, of feeling my own blood sloshing around in my mouth, and learning to recover fast enough to not get hit again was something that I had not been prepared for by anything I had read. And when I did manage to get a kick in, what surprised me was just how much it hurt me. That was my first experience of how theory sometimes leaves you unprepared for the real world.

Many years later, I had a similar experience with marketing. I loved the classes in business school, read all I could on the subject, and without a second thought took up my dream job—brand management at Procter & Gamble. Now, almost a dozen years later, I love marketing more than ever, but I realize that marketing is just like karate—you can read all about it, but nothing really prepares you for the chaos of the real world, where unpredictable competitors, fast changing markets, demanding bosses and finicky consumers make marketing theory alone a very bad way of preparing for a career in marketing or understanding what the real world of brand management is like.

This book is no substitute for the various great books on marketing and management theory you can find, but it aims to complement them with some lessons from the trenches of brand management. Specifically, I hope it gives a flavor of how theories and concepts can be applied in the real world to build great and enduring brands. I cannot claim to provide an exhaustive listing of every single issue that marketers face, but have tried to capture many of the common challenges a marketer encounters in the real world. Also, I hope this book gives you some exposure to that critical "P" of marketing that most books do not mention—people. Marketing is at best an inexact science, and its application and results depend to a large extent on the motivations, skills and relationships of the people involved.

As I said, I am no theorist, but I have taken my share of blows in the sparring ring of marketing, and this book is meant to give you a flavor of what that tastes like.

Let the lessons begin.

Mainak Dhar

POSITIONING

Advertising may be described as the science of arresting the human intelligence long enough to get money from it.

- Stephen Leacock

As a student of marketing, positioning was something that always fascinated me. In many ways, it was the "purest" aspect of marketing: trying to slot your brand into your consumer's mind in a way that differentiates it from the competition. The strategic choices involved in this are usually the bedrock for all the other elements of the marketing mix. So while it may be impossible to say which "P" of marketing is the most important, it is a pretty easy choice when it comes to deciding which one to start with. In the real world, positioning continues to be one of the most exciting aspects of marketing, due in part to the fact that you are operating in a dynamic context where your competitors are not going to sit back and let you occupy the most desirable position in your consumer's mind. Also, while the basic principles of positioning that you learned in textbooks may still largely hold true, their application in the real world needs to be modified depending on where your brand is in its life cycle. A new launch requires different thinking compared to an effort to grow a large, established brand; similarly, growing a successful brand requires slightly different approaches compared to trying to turn around one that is in deep trouble.

This section of the book will give you some pointers on how you can create a desirable positioning for your brand, defend against competitive moves, adapt to changing market situations, and think about extending a brand's positioning across categories or segments.

Building a better mousetrap: Creating new ideas and concepts

One of the most exciting, and most terrifying, things a young marketer is often asked to do is to come up with a new idea—whether it be for an event, a promotion or the launch of a new product. It is exciting because this is the reason that most people join marketing in the first place: to feel the stimulation of ideation and then the thrill of seeing one's creation come alive in the marketplace. I do not have any kids yet, but when I saw the first ad on which I had worked broadcast on TV, I felt like jumping and shouting to the world, "That's my baby!"

Oh, did I mention terrifying? Terrifying because, more often than not, such critical tasks filter down to the most junior and inexperienced team members, who are often still struggling with their other tasks of locating the washroom and tracking down the coffee machine. Inexperience, enthusiasm, fear of screwing up and a burning desire to prove oneself combine to form the cocktail that sustains most young marketers as they start their careers. It would be pretentious to say that I can summarize all that you need to know about this in a few glib sentences, but I'll share some thoughts to get you started on this critical building block in positioning a brand: deciding what you want the brand to stand for.

Mix 50% inspiration and 50% perspiration—Ideation is a science and an art

Let me start with a little quiz. Assume you are asked to come up with the idea for the positioning of a new brand of beer that is being launched in the market. Which of these most accurately describes how you would get started on coming up with the idea?

a) Ask for data on existing beer brands and consumers; analyze what current brands offer and what consumers want in an ideal beer, and try and find a gap in the market—either in terms of some key needs not being met, or a consumer segment that no brand is currently talking to.

b) Go to the nearest pub with a friend, and while trying out several brands of beer so you see and taste firsthand what is available in the market, bounce around ideas and come up with something that sounds like it could be new and exciting.

So, what is the right answer? In my book, you should probably do both! A lot of people immerse themselves in data, trying to find a neat intellectual solution to marketing issues. Do not get me wrong, nothing beats having all of the data concerning your category and your consumer; however, by itself, this is usually not enough. That is simply because marketing in real life is not an abstract intellectual challenge or a business school case study to be solved in the vacuum of one's room, but rather it is a dynamic problem involving ever-changing variables, and you never know where a new insight could come from. In addition, data tend to reflect what exists, not possibilities that consumers have not yet articulated. Therefore, there is usually no substitute for "getting one's hands dirty" by meeting consumers, visiting stores for inspiration, and experiencing the market in the flesh, rather than on sheets of paper or on one's computer screen.

As an example, the idea for a global brand that has sales of hundreds of millions of dollars came from a chance observation from watching women make *sake* in Japan. The observation (the inspiration) was that the women working in the brewery had unnaturally smooth hands. This seemingly irrelevant observation led to intense research (the perspiration) that studied the chemical processes involved, and identified an agent that had such an effect on skin. That agent came to be known as Pitera, and the brand that emerged out of this flash of inspiration was SK-II.

A breakthrough insight can come in either order—a chance observation like the one above, followed by detailed analysis and validation; or a process of data analysis to generate hypotheses or ideas that are then backed up by real world observation. It really does not matter in which order you approach it, as long as you remember to leave yourself open to some inspiration.

LESSON 2:
I know they want it, but who else offers it? Differentiate, don't imitate

Chances are that when you were in school or college, you had a crush on someone. Now imagine that you are back in school, and that you have found out that this certain special person has two passions, watching football and reading poetry. One of the people trying to ask her out (no offense to readers, but I am assigning genders for simplicity) is the football captain, who is a real jock but is far from a literary genius. You, on the other hand, are quite well read, but you are more likely to trip over the ball than score a goal. So what do you do?

a) Brush up on your football skills so you can try out for the team and impress her on the field.

b) Dust off your books of poetry and, next time you meet her, see if you do indeed have some common ground to build upon.

The answer seems blindingly obvious, doesn't it? But you would be surprised how such common sense sometimes eludes marketers in the real world, who somehow believe that they can win just by offering what consumers want, without looking at whether some competitor already offers it. This is usually justified by delusions of "our product is better," "our marketing is better," or, the biggest delusion of them all, "our people are better." Now, which soft drink brand comes to mind when I say "new generation"? Which entertainment brand comes to mind when I say "family fun"? Pepsi and Disney are just two great examples of brands that own a positioning first in consumers' minds. There are many other types of cola out there and many other media companies, but it would be tough for them to take over these leading positions, even if their cola tastes better or their programming is better liked.

The point is simple: it is good to be better, but it's better to be different. Just as in our example above, the consumer's mind already has one "brand" that owns the positioning of "football ace," and trying to dislodge this existing competitor is not likely to do much for your love life, although it may well improve your tackling skills. On the other hand, "reads poetry in spare time" is an open positioning that you could be the first to fill, and it is also something in which your competitor would have difficulty matching you.

LESSON 3:
Remember that everyone wants free ice cream! Learn to be selective

Do you like ice cream? If not, then substitute beer, chocolate or whatever it is that you like a lot. Suppose I were to ask you choose between one scoop or two scoops of ice cream for the same price. What would you choose? I do think it is reasonable to assume that most people would gladly take the extra serving.

Now if I were to tell you that for the extra scoop you would have to pay 50% more. What would you do? Chances are that more people would say yes the first time around than would say yes to the second offer. This goes to show that when people do not know there is an extra cost involved, more is usually better.

The flip side holds equally true for marketers when they do not recognize the costs involved in bundling too many benefits or attributes, and automatically assume that more is better. This cost to marketers can be in the form of an unsustainable cost structure that leads to higher prices and poor consumer value, or simply in the form of an excessively diffused positioning such that the brand does not really end up standing for anything. What usually makes such "more is better" thinking prevalent is that a lot of decisions are based on consumer research in which consumers do not actually have to pay money or do not have the option of choosing a competitive offering. As a lot of marketers have learned the hard way, there is a huge difference between consumers ticking "will definitely buy" on a market research questionnaire and consumers actually shelling out money for a product when cheaper competitive options exist, albeit without some of the frills.

The point here is not that it is always necessary to sell products cheaply, but rather that it is important to understand what you really want to stand for in the consumer's mind, and then to structure the proposition or product to convey that message as strongly as possible. A good example of this is McDonald's, which is able to offer speed, convenience and affordability by limiting frills like table-side service and minimizing customized offerings. I can bet you that if you conducted a market research test in which everything that McDonald's offers was combined with table-side service, no standing in queues and the ability to customize food ("I'd like less mayo and more mustard on my burger, please"), you would get higher purchase intent. However, the reality is that translating this finding into the real world would likely be suicide from both a cost standpoint (the added staffing and inventory costs) and a brand equity standpoint (if you want fine dining, why would you go to a McDonald's anyway?).

Breaching the defenses: Sourcing market share from an existing player

Everybody loves an underdog. There is something very attractive about the struggle in the David vs. Goliath story that usually leads us to root for the little guy, the dark horse, the weaker team, when they face seemingly impossible odds. No wonder there are so many movies based on such a theme. Marketers are no exception. I think most marketers fantasize about working on a brand that wins against a huge competitor, where they can prove their mettle against the odds, and sheer marketing brilliance helps them succeed where all others have failed. Unfortunately, in the real world, more often that not, the big brand steps all over the small challenger. There are certainly exceptions, but this tends to happen only when the smaller brand plays by certain rules.

LESSON 4:
Aim small, hit hard—Attack on a narrow front

Yes, David beat Goliath, but have you wondered what would have happened if he had challenged Goliath to a wrestling match? I don't know about you, but my money would be on Goliath. In essence, David applied a lesson that is equally valid for marketers today. If you are up against a much bigger competitor, you are better off not to engage him in all-out frontal combat. The key is to find a point of vulnerability and then focus your attack there; in David's case, with a slingshot.

In marketing terms, this means that when you study a large competitor, the trick is not to try to "out shout" it, but rather to find a segment of its customers with a higher appeal for you, or to find some benefits you can offer that it does not, and then focus all of your marketing on this consumer segment and offering. In practical terms, ask yourself (and your research agency) "which segment of competitive users is likely to convert to me first?" Once you know this, see how you can design your plans to attract this segment to your brand. When you have built some scale and made some inroads, you can think about challenging the competitor more head-on, but to start with, ruthless focus is the best way to stay alive against a much larger competitor. First, starting with a focused, less direct competitive approach allows you to develop a foothold in the consumer's mind from which to launch a broader challenge. Second, a larger competitor may not react as violently to a narrow attack as it would to an all-out attack. The gut reaction of a marketer working on a large, established brand, when faced with a frontal attack by a smaller competitor, is to crush it before it becomes a bigger threat. On the other hand, a narrower attack that nibbles away at market share may be ignored until it is already too late.

This point is valid even if you are a large player. Whatever your company's size, finding narrow segments where you can tap new users without head-on competition can be a smart and less bloody way of building scale. This scenario plays out all of the time in the real-world marketplace. In the gaming console wars, for example, the slugging match between Sony's PlayStation franchise and Microsoft's Xbox has been hogging much of the headlines. However, even as Sony takes on Microsoft in open battle in this segment, it has also launched the extremely successful PSP handheld gaming device. The PSP device taps into a unique segment where Microsoft does not compete by addressing a specific consumer need—mobile gaming—while the PlayStation franchise continues to face the Xbox juggernaut in the mainstream gaming console market.

LESSON 5:
Judo not sumo: Use competitive strengths against them

When looking at competitors, we often tend to think of all the things they may do, building elaborate SWOT (strength, weakness, opportunity and threat) charts in an attempt to read the competitors' minds. This is undeniably useful, but sometimes the key to winning against an entrenched competitor is to ask the opposite question: "What would my competitor never do?" One of the inherent disadvantages of a large brand is its own strength—mass appeal means that it must appeal to very diverse segments and end up being many things to many people. For a small brand challenging a large, existing player, the answer often lies in turning this strength to a weakness by focusing on a narrow segment or positioning where the existing player will not follow for fear of alienating its current user base. This is something with which you are probably already familiar, as such concepts have been covered in several marketing texts. What I will do, however, is give some practical tips on how you can translate this to action in the real world.

A good way to put this into practice is to take all that you know about your competitors and put yourself in their shoes. Imagine that you are running their business and ask yourself what you would not do for fear of diluting "your" brand equity or losing your current users. This seemingly simple exercise often yields critical insights into how you can position your brand in the minds of competitive users. A second trick, once again putting yourself in your competitors' place, is to profile "your" users and categorize those who are the most loyal users and those who are most likely to move to other brands. This would give you a good starting point on which to focus your efforts.

Now back to our school crush scenario. If you had any doubts about the wisdom of not trying to compete on the football field and out-jock the jock, ask yourself what he would never do. I am guessing he would not want to be seen hanging around the library too much. Does this give you any ideas about where you could approach your object of desire without fear of your competition stealing your thunder?

Make an offer they can't refuse—
Understand and break down their barriers

Assume that you have taken the lessons thus far to heart and have identified a segment of consumers that you want your brand to target with a single-minded proposition, and in a way that encourages consumers to try your brand without attracting a competitive onslaught. So, what do you do now? Sit back and wait for the fruits of your marketing genius to roll in? Hardly. Just because you know whom you want to sell to and what you want to sell does not actually mean that they will buy. This is when you need to anticipate and understand what barriers may prevent your targeted consumers from trying your brand, and then develop a plan to bust through these obstacles.

The key to success is to identify the obstacles beforehand and to have a plan that attacks them head-on. The nature of the barrier, and how best to bust it, will differ from category to category and market to market, but the principle is the same. In a real-world marketing context, this can be achieved through a simple exercise of hypothesis setting.

In general, busting barriers is primarily a question of risk minimization. Every decision, whether to buy a car, choose an airline, or date someone, comes with an associated risk. This risk may be monetary ("this car is much more expensive than the other, and I do not know if it is worth the extra money"), physical ("I have heard that this airline has a terrible safety record") or emotional ("I am not sure that I am ready to commit to a relationship"). So ask yourself one question: What would make your target consumer perceive that there is less risk in choosing your brand? A great example of a brand that has done this is Dove. In beauty care, a common barrier is consumer cynicism ("everybody looks beautiful in advertising, but how do I know your product really works?"). Using a successful combination of a "women like you" testimonial campaign and offering "before-your-eyes proof" through simple devices like the litmus test, Dove has built a huge global brand in a brutally competitive market.

Enemy at the gates: Defending against competitive attack

The last lesson was all about attacking an existing player, while this one is about the reverse—how to defend when you are under attack. Imagine that you are fast asleep at home, after a great dinner with your family. In the dead of night, you hear a strange noise in the living room. You check it out and realize there is an intruder in your home! How would you feel?

Angry at this invasion of your space? Afraid of something happening to you or your loved ones?

In real life, facing a major competitive attack evokes similar reactions among marketers. Leave aside all you learned in business school about how marketers react to competition. When the competition comes calling and you happen to be near a brand team, the first thing you will hear is not a rational discussion about SWOTs or principles gleaned from marketing texts on competitive advantage. Chances are the first things you will hear are a few choice four-letter words and a lot of emotional reactions. That is why reacting to a competitive act can be very dangerous, as it is usually not a cold and rational decision, but rather one tinged with plenty of emotion and adrenaline.

Know who blinks first—Understand the broader strategic stakes

We are back in your home when you have discovered the intruder. I am going to give you some more information about this intruder. Let's see how that influences your reaction. First, suppose the intruder is an unarmed 10-year-old child from a poor family who has never committed a crime before and who has broken into your home to steal some easy money to buy Nike shoes. What would you do?

Now suppose the intruder is a serial offender with a long prison record for violent offenses, and who has been stalking your family all evening. Would you approach the situation any differently? I don't know about you, but in the first case, I would probably just interrupt him and try to scare him away. In the second, I would not just call the cops, but also find something that could serve as a weapon and be ready to strike the first blow in case I had to confront him. If I tried the former strategy with the second type of intruder, I would probably be seriously hurt, as would my family. On the other hand, taking an overly aggressive approach with the small child would be a huge overreaction and I would probably find myself in legal trouble for causing serious harm to the child.

It is the same in marketing: it is critical that you know what the stakes are for your competitor. Is your competitor just fishing for quick gains, and will back off in the face of a determined defense? Or is it playing for keeps, and you have a bloodbath on your hands that you cannot avoid? In the example above, you probably would not have any of the background information, but in facing a competitive attack on your brand, you can equip yourself with some pretty good clues as to your competitor's intent. Your finance department can often assist by helping you identify profit pockets for you and your competition, as well as the broader strategic imperatives for both companies. This would help you understand just how deep your competitor's pockets are. For example, if your competitor has other large, profitable businesses, especially ones where you do not compete, chances are it may be able and willing to plow in significant investments against your brand.

A great example is again from the gaming console market, where the Xbox launch was clearly a long-term play by Microsoft to enter this segment, where it could afford to invest heavily in the short term due to its profitable base business. Microsoft's competitors in this segment, Sony and Nintendo, were unable to nullify this scale advantage, since they could do nothing to attack many of Microsoft's profit pockets, such as its software business.

LESSON 8:
Play to the home crowd—Protect your loyal users first

In the home invasion scenario, your first instinct would probably be to protect the safety of your family. You would probably get them locked away in a room while you called the police, or, if you had to, confronted the intruder. Once again, marketing is all about applying the same common sense thinking to business. In a competitive attack situation, the first thing you should do is protect your loyal users. Too often, in the fog of competitive reaction and counter-reaction, the attention shifts to what the competitor is doing and how to counter it, rather than focusing on hunkering down and making sure your current users do not have an incentive to shift.

Part of the game is to turn Lesson 6 on its head and increase the perceived risk of shifting to a new brand by either playing up the familiarity and heritage of your brand or the perceived unfamiliarity of the challenger. Another part of the strategy is to simply load up your current users for the initial window of vulnerability when the competitor launches. It may not sound like sexy marketing, but never underestimate the power of a simple price-off or a "Buy x, get y free" offer to load up your current users and take them out of the market, thereby preventing them from shifting to a new competitor. Timing is key: if you do it too late, your users would already have been in the market and possibly tried the competitor. A rule of thumb is to try to remove your users from the market for at least one purchase cycle. This strategy is second nature in fast-moving consumer goods (FMCG) categories like beauty care or foods, but it is equally relevant for other contexts. Examples of this strategy in use include scenarios like a bank offering discounted rates on loans when new competitors launch, or an airline offering special privileges to its frequent flyers when new airlines start encroaching on its routes.

In addition to such tactical moves, when you are under serious attack from a dangerous competitor, it may be worthwhile to tailor all elements of your marketing mix to protect your loyal users. That may mean supporting lines or flavors that are most purchased by your loyal users or shifting your in-store money to channels where these users tend to shop most.

LESSON 9:
Raise the stakes—Make the cost of victory too much to bear

Suppose you do have to confront the intruder—what objective do you have in mind? I would say forget what you have seen in the movies where the good guy pummels the bad guy into submission. I would settle for the intruder backing off and running away, and leaving my family and me alone. Most books will tell you that unless you happen to be dealing with the very small minority of serial killers and psychopaths, most criminals will back off when they face determined resistance, since getting hurt is not something they have bargained for. If you corner the intruder and give him no room to escape, you are probably making things worse, not better, since he will have no option but to fight. In other words, the objective is not to fight, but rather to make it clear that you are not a pushover and that this will not be a painless conquest.

In the world of marketing, too often you hear young brand managers say things like "We'll wipe them out," or "We'll put them out of business." Brave words, but usually stupid words if they are backed by action and money, since in the real world you will rarely put a competitor out of business through a competitive defense. It may work in the rare situation where you are the overwhelming leader, and the challenger is a smaller player with no other profit pockets. If you have followed Lesson 7, you will know whether this is the case, or if your competitor is here to stay, with profits from other categories to plow into this launch. In the latter case, fantasies of wiping them out will likely remain just that. The more pragmatic strategy may be to estimate how much they are willing to lose and how much you can lose, and then to make this a war of attrition where you can demonstrate your willingness and ability to stand your ground. I firmly believe that it is better to defend fiercely to save your current business than to embark upon the infinitely more costly exercise of trying to woo back consumers who have already shifted to a competitor. Defending your current client base may require actions such as shoring up your media to competitive levels, implementing aggressive promotions and increasing in-store displays.

In parallel, a strategy that will increase the cost to competitors of challenging your brand would be to threaten their profit pockets. In this situation, knowledge of where your competitors make money and how they plan to fund their launch will once again be invaluable. If the intruder knew his own house had just caught fire, chances are he would be hurrying back to save his home!

There are no limits to growth: Growing a high market share brand

Conventional wisdom says that the bigger a business gets, the tougher it is to keep growing at the same pace. That may well be true in most cases, and if you look over a long time horizon—say 20 years—there will be only a handful of brands still leading their categories after such a long time. But then there are the truly iconic brands—take Coca-Cola, Pampers or McDonald's, for example—which have not just endured, but have found ways to reinvent themselves and continue growing in the face of new competitors, changing consumer trends and market realities. So, it is not impossible for a large brand to keep growing, it is just a matter of knowing what it takes to keep growing over the long term.

LESSON 10:
Would you like fries with that? Use the magic of driving consumption

If marketers thought more like entrepreneurs running their own business, they would have more intuitive answers to a lot of the business issues they face because they would rely more on their instincts and common sense rather than approaching problems as purely intellectual exercises. I like to frame marketing issues through analogies that put one "on the spot," thinking like an entrepreneur would. So, suppose you were to open a restaurant that sold burgers and soft drinks. You do roaring business for some time as customer after customer laps up your burgers. One day, you realize that your sales growth has started flattening because, let's face it, there is a limit to how many burgers a person can eat, and you have attracted as many new customers in your area as you can. What would you do? Write down three ideas that come to mind.

I am guessing you may have had several wacky ideas, but one of them may have been to try convincing existing customers to eat at your restaurant on more occasions. If people largely come to the restaurant for dinner, how could you get some people to come for breakfast or lunch? The second approach to increasing sales would be to get them to spend more on each dining occasion by increasing the size of burgers or by adding to the range of items available on each consumption occasion (e.g. adding starters, fries or desserts to your menu). If your ideas included these, you would fit right in at McDonald's, as its continued growth for many years was based on this strategy.

Both approaches essentially operate on the same principle: increasing the "share of wallet" among existing customers by either finding new consumption occasions or increasing the amount of your brand that they consume per occasion. Both are proven ways for a large, existing brand to continue fueling its growth. So, next time you try to justify why your brand is not growing by saying that it is already too big, ask yourself two simple questions:

a) Is there one more occasion where my brand could be used where it is not currently used?

b) Is there a way that I could get my consumer to use more of my brand per usage occasion?

LESSON 11:
Start a retrial factory—Continually seek new users

The other trick to continue growing is to define success as finding new users. In the example above, the logical next phase of growth would be to open more outlets in your town, then perhaps expand to other towns, and, who knows, one day expand to other countries altogether.

Geographical expansion is a proven way of growing a brand by tapping into new users in all sorts of industries, from banking to fast food. Yes, there will theoretically be a time when you run out of people to market to, but over the short to medium term, expansion into new consumer markets and segments almost always works.

You may ask the question: "Geographical expansion is easy, but what if I have to operate in only one market and I do not have this easy way out?" The answer is that the same basic principle applies. Is there a group of consumers not using your brand today to which you could expand your appeal? You could arrive at such opportunities in any number of ways, slicing consumers by demographics, gender, life stage or income. Any of them may work—the key is to know which may be right for your category and brand, and to look at how well your brand is penetrated in each segment. This should expose some potential segments where your brand is under-represented today.

One of the most successful examples of this in recent times has been Gillette's expansion into the female segment. Long known as the gold standard in male shaving products, Gillette identified a potential growth opportunity among females. Gillette found that while the functional need was similar (hair removal) and they could fully leverage their technical expertise, the basic emotional need was very different among men and women. For men, shaving is one of the integral parts of their grooming routine and a key part of feeling masculine. For women, shaving is the removal of something unwanted that comes in the way of them fully revealing their femininity. What resulted was an exercise in classic marketing, spanning the creation of a totally new brand, revolutionary design to appeal to this new target consumer, and a new proposition that resonated among female shavers ("Unveil the goddess in you"). The resulting brand, Venus, has become a huge global success and a great example of how a brand was able to identify and tap into a new set of consumers to continue fuelling growth.

LESSON 12:
Seek new horizons—Reframe and refresh the competitive set

What business do you think Nike is in? Shoes? Think again. If Nike had defined its business just the way it had started, it would be nowhere close to where it is now in terms of ubiquity and sales. Along the way, Nike redefined the need it fulfilled from merely offering footwear to providing authentic athletic performance. Doing so opened up a wide range of growth opportunities for the brand, from apparel to sponsorships to sports equipment. That is the hallmark of a truly great brand—the ability to see beyond the obvious physical need that it meets, and then find a broader set of needs that it can tap into to keep growing the brand. One of my close friends is a loyal Starbucks consumer—he starts each day with a latte—but his loyalty goes beyond just the physical need for good coffee. He collects Starbucks mugs from every city he visits and drinks coffee at home from these mugs, trying to recreate the "Starbucks experience" when he cannot be there. This kind of loyalty is something every brand would envy, and it would never have emerged if Starbucks had limited its vision to just selling a good cup of coffee.

Ask yourself what other needs, both physical and emotional, your consumers are seeking to fulfill when they interact with your brand. That one question can unlock a whole set of possibilities, since you may find yourself competing with a whole new set of products and services. A Harley-Davidson buyer, for example, does not just want the means to get from point A to point B, but also wants the feeling of control and power and the pride of being associated with a certain elite group. For Harley owners, their motorcycle plays a role in creating their personal identity, which they proudly display to the world. That is why you can recognize Harley owners even when they are nowhere near their bikes: their trademark tattoos, caps and leather vests are meant to show off who they are. This kind of relationship between brands and consumers is not just limited to ultra-premium and prestigious brands. Disney was able to evolve from a straightforward cartoon company into a multi-billion dollar empire by expanding its positioning to "wholesome family entertainment," which led it to compete in categories like entertainment parks, movies and toys.

Sounds easy, doesn't it? Well, before you become too excited, remember that for every Disney or Starbucks, there are hundreds of brands that have tried to expand their horizons and failed miserably, even when the parent brand itself was very strong. The next chapter will show you how to build an empire for your brand.

Empire-building: The mega-branding challenge

The problem with most empires in human history is that they tend to overextend themselves, and this condition, termed "imperial overreach" by historians, becomes the root cause of the empire's decline. Brands are no different. For a lot of brands, extending the core equity too far and into too many categories becomes an important cause of decline. The reason for this behavior is something that empire builders and brand managers have in common: a seemingly unquenchable thirst for growth. This chapter aims to share some lessons on the delicate balancing act between seeking perpetual growth for a brand by identifying new segments and categories to play in, and extending a brand so far that it breaks.

LESSON 13:
Create value, not just volume—Seek competency and equity fit, not just added sales

The temptation to extend into a new category is great when the potential for new users and volume seems huge. In the short term, you may well achieve some added sales, but the difference between success and failure lies in answering two questions:

1. Does this new segment or category allow you to leverage some things you are currently good at in terms of marketing, manufacturing or distribution?

2. Is your existing brand equity an advantage when entering this new category?

In the Gillette-Venus example, Gillette could fully tap into its existing manufacturing and distribution expertise. Also, its equity as the gold standard in men's shaving products was a huge advantage while it grappled with the challenge of targeting a new set of consumers. In the last chapter, I mentioned how Starbucks has been able to tap into needs and categories beyond its starting point, but even a great brand like Starbucks faces natural limits to how far it can stretch itself.

Imagine that Starbucks were to start a new chain called Starbucks Pizza. Would you go there instead of your regular Pizza Hut? I would venture to say that Starbucks Pizza would have a tough time. On the one hand, it would have some existing skills it could draw on in terms of running food and beverage outlets, such as the necessary service skills and training procedures. On the other hand is the fact that Starbucks' current equity (a great coffee experience) would not readily translate into this new category, no matter how tasty the pizzas.

LESSON 14:
Would you play football without shoes? Learn the rules of the game in each category

Even if you have found a category to extend your brand into that seems to be perfect in terms of equity fit, it does not mean success is assured. Let me use another analogy: suppose an Olympic swimmer were to try his hand at football. He would have some obvious advantages that would help him in his new sport, such as great physical condition, discipline and the proven ability to perform under pressure. Of course, he would have to learn the basics of the sport, but you'd assume that he'd have a huge head start over any ordinary person starting out in the sport. Now the big day arrives, and our star arrives on the field without the proper shoes. All his superb physical condition and training aside, all that he would likely achieve is a serious foot injury. This is because no matter how well he may have otherwise performed, he ignored some of the basic rules of the game.

It is the same in marketing. When you choose to extend your brand to a new category, you need to act with a bit of humility and put aside how strong your brand may be in the category where it plays today. You need to be willing to learn and play by the rules of the new category you are entering, which could have implications regarding the marketing and distribution models needed to succeed or the basic product or design features consumers expect in that category. If you want to avoid getting bloody feet like our aspiring football player, there are some basic issues that you need to address to see if you are ready to play by the rules of any new category or segment. These include consumer media habits and how they may be different from those of your parent brand's consumers; the nature of distribution channels; and the type and pace of innovation needed to win in this new segment. What sometimes makes this difficult is the human tendency to operate within one's "comfort zone" and fall back on what one is good at or finds familiar. As a result, when brands are extended into a new segment or category, the temptation is to run this new part of the business in the same way that the mother brand is run. However, what is often critical for success in extending a brand is understanding what is likely to be different, and then being able to adapt to it. In the Starbucks Pizza example, this may entail developing capabilities like home delivery, which is not a core part of the current Starbucks business model but is considered the norm in the pizza business.

LESSON 15:
Create a recurring deposit—Pay back into parent brand equity

One of the things smart empire builders have had in common throughout history, from the Romans to the British, is the foresight to use their colonies to augment the motherland's resources. This took the form of natural resources, money from taxation and the formation of large professional armies that did battle for the empire around the world. This approach was one of the reasons why a small island nation like Britain could dominate so much of the world. If it had relied solely on an army comprising its own citizens, it would have overreached itself much more quickly and collapsed sooner.

It is the same with branding, in terms of making sure that the new category you want to expand your brand into does something to augment your total brand equity and scale. So even if you have successfully expanded your brand into a new category or segment, it is important to ensure that playing in this new segment not only generates added sales, but also does something to enhance the total brand equity. That is when mega-branding really yields a multiplier effect—when the presence in multiple categories exponentially builds what the total brand stands for.

A great example is Dove, which has carried with it across multiple categories some key brand equities, such as a common moisturizing property in its products and the brand's blue and white color palette. This has ensured that no matter which category the brand has expanded into, each expansion has added to Dove's total equity—and this has paid off in unimaginable synergies in their go-to-market strategy. For instance, when Dove launched into the hair care segment, it was able to piggyback on its skin care business to get quick trial and distribution.

To do this, you need to start with a very clear understanding of what lies at the core of your brand. Just as people pick up new mannerisms and habits over time, brands tend to accumulate additional attributes and benefits as they extend across categories. To get to what may be the very core of your brand, it may be a good exercise to spend some time with your most loyal users and understand what makes them stick to your brand. Doing so may yield some clues as to what aspects of your brand you ought to protect as sacrosanct even as you expand it to far horizons.

Miracles do happen: Turning around a declining brand

Imagine you could choose the brand that you work on. Would it not be great if you could work on the brand that is the darling of top management, one that has been growing year on year, one where you have all the resources you need to keep taking the brand to even greater success? Now pinch yourself, rub your eyes and wake up to the cruel reality that in the course of any career as a marketer, there will inevitably be times when the brand you work on is the ugly duckling and not the belle of the ball. So what do you do? Curse your fate, resign yourself to a couple of years of your career down the tube, and wait for the moment when you can get reassigned to a brand that is in better shape?

You could, but you would not be doing yourself any favors. I have yet to meet a marketer who says, "I want my brand's sales to decline." Turning around a declining brand can be the most exciting thing you ever do as a marketer, and it is an experience that teaches you a lot about both marketing and leadership.

Shaken and stirred—Call out a crisis, it's not business as usual!

In 79 AD, one of the biggest cities in the Roman Empire lay shattered and covered in smoldering lava, its once mighty buildings buried along with thousands of its citizens. Hundreds of years later, as scientists excavated the ruins of Pompeii, one of the remarkable things they found was that many of the victims seemed to have died doing perfectly ordinary things—eating, sleeping in their beds, taking a bath. It is almost as if many of them were oblivious to the imminent disaster, even though they would have seen the volcano smoking for at least a few days and the area had witnessed earthquakes for years. The explanation for their behavior lies in the fact that most people try to wish problems away, assuming that things will somehow work out. I am not a shrink, but it may be because nobody wants to look silly like the boy who cried wolf. In marketing, even though a brand may seem to be obviously in trouble, with declining sales or equities, quite often people working on it will try to find explanations for this rather than confront it as the imminent crisis that it is. As a marketer faced with such a situation, your first job is to light a fire under people's seats and shake them out of complacency. It takes courage, as you do run the risk of overstating what may indeed be a short-term issue, but often it is better than waiting to see your brand, and your career, buried under a disaster.

The first step of turning around a brand in trouble is not to apply some smart frameworks or analysis, but to get the team working on the brand to rally around a common understanding of the issue and put them into crisis mode to commit to fixing it. This sounds intuitive and like a lot of common sense, but then that is what marketing is usually all about. This first step is important because a crisis brings about different behaviors, decisions and actions than when it is business as usual. Some important initial steps include:

1. Quickly pinpoint what is the core issue you are trying to solve. When a business is in trouble, the tendency to try to fix everything is a natural temptation. You need to focus the thinking on what the real issue is: is it declining trial, is distribution a problem, or is there a product issue?

2. Assemble a team to work on it as a priority apart from their regular responsibilities. Everyone usually becomes so preoccupied with their "day jobs" that they rarely have time to really step back and return to

fundamentals—something you need to do in a crisis.

3. Identify key questions to be addressed and the dates and milestones by which they will be tackled. When things are going downhill, you cannot afford to let things drift.

4. Let your bosses know all of the above. In a real-world business crisis, your bosses will be all too eager to "help," and sometimes management attention is not a good thing. Attention from management can distract your crisis team from working on the issues they need to look at, and with the business in trouble, the added stress of management questions is something that nobody needs. Informing your bosses early on and updating them regularly will give them the confidence that you are on top of things, and this will hopefully get them off your back while you figure out how to sort things out.

LESSON 17:

Look at the bright side—what do you have to lose anyway? Think big, not incrementally

Okay, now you have everyone all worked up about turning around your brand. So, what do you do? When your brand is faced with a real crisis, continuing to do what you usually do instead of tackling the core issues involved is often a recipe for disaster. Tinkering around with a few new pieces of advertising when the brand has a basic product performance or value issue is likely to be as effective as rearranging the deck chairs on the Titanic when it was bearing down on the iceberg. So what do you do?

Before jumping to the answer, it is worthwhile to consider why people in crisis situations often continue to do what is normally done and yet hope for different results. I suspect that the answer lies in the fear of loss. It is the same reason why people hesitate to intervene when they see a stranger being mugged on the street, and why governments hesitate to take economic decisions that are right but may result in the alienation of voters. The fear of losing something we value—safety, money or power— is a powerful self-preservation instinct that kicks in at times of crisis. And that is the instinct you will have to fight to succeed when you face the task of turning around a brand.

There is no easy way to do it, but here are a few thoughts on the subject. First, remember that when the brand is in decline, you are probably up against a low base for next year's results! So on the bright side, if you do not totally screw things up, it is hard to do worse. That tends to be a liberating thought to overcome the real and very legitimate fear of losing out in one's career. The other trick that I have seen work if you are dealing with a small brand is to imagine that you have withdrawn the brand and are launching it again. Encourage yourself and your team to think this way and also convince your management that this is the spirit in which you want them to look at your plans. That liberates you to think afresh on getting the fundamentals right instead of worrying about losing whatever little business you have today. The final thought in such a situation is to try to get some new members on your team to help look at the situation. When the team is composed of the same people who were involved when the problems afflicting your brand began, it may be difficult to get radical new thinking. This is simply because people do not like admitting that they screwed up! So avoid this trap by getting a fresh perspective on the situation. Just remember that it is better for you to acknowledge what may have gone wrong and recommend drastic changes than it is for your management to reach the same conclusion and change the brand manager!

LESSON 18:
Remember the other "P" of marketing: Patience!

As you read this book, one of the things that will irritate you is that some of the lessons are easy to share, but much harder to adopt in real life. I liken it to a friend telling you after you have been dumped that over time, you will forget him or her and move on. You know it is true, but when you hear it you feel like shouting at your friend that it is easier to give advice than to go through what you are dealing with. This is one of those frustrating lessons: if you want to turn around a brand, do not expect overnight miracles. It will likely be a hard slog, and there will be months, and perhaps years, when it looks like things are not going to improve. Here are some thoughts to help you cope while you wait.

1. Set realistic expectations. If a brand does need radical surgery such as a total re-positioning, results will take time to come through. So if business does not turn around in a few months, do not assume all is lost. Setting unrealistic expectations of success is a sure way to set yourself up for disappointment.

2. Have some milestones that you can look forward to and use to measure success. While a total turnaround may take time, there will always be signs that will tell you if you are on the right track. It could

be research results saying that consumers love your new proposition, favorable responses to new packaging, or early signs of business recovery. Whatever the indicators, know and measure them to ensure that you are making progress.

3. Celebrate all the small victories along the way, such as when you hit one of the above milestones. When business is tough, what the team often needs is the encouragement to keep going. For a brand that is growing 10% year on year, a flat performance versus a year ago would be nothing to write home about. However, for a brand in terminal decline, it could be the sign that you are about to turn the corner. Recognizing and celebrating moments like these could be the difference between a team that hangs in there and one which abandons what looks like a sinking ship.

A brand new you: Reinventing and relaunching an existing brand

While turning around a brand is an opportunity that may come your way only rarely in the course of your career, something you are sure to encounter more often is the relaunching of an existing brand. A restage, or relaunch, has several definitions, but for the purposes of this book, let us define it as any activity that aims to make consumers reconsider a brand in its totality versus the launch of individual items or lines. This could be through packaging changes, product upgrades, a new positioning, or any combination of several changes in the fundamentals of the brand. There are many reasons why a brand could be relaunched, including the availability of new technology, a desire to upgrade a dated image, or competitive actions. Whatever the reason, relaunches are common, but experience in the real world indicates that failed relaunches are even more common.

To understand why, let us take another analogy from everyday life. Assume you are trying to win over a major new client, and you think it may be a good idea to get to know the client team better outside of work. They are the same age as you, but they are a tight bunch, with common interests like golf, theater and spending their evenings enjoying fine wine. You, on the other hand, have always been more of a "regular Joe," whose idea of evening entertainment is a beer with your buddies. So what do you do? In answering that we can learn a lot about what it takes to create a successful relaunch.

LESSON 19:

When familiarity does not breed contempt—Learn the importance of keeping loyal users

In the example above, let us assume that you pick up golf, change from jeans into formal clothes, and finally learn the proper form for sipping wine. You may or may not fit in with your clients, but one thing is for sure: your old buddies would find you very odd indeed. It is the same with many relaunches—in trying to go after new users, brand managers often forget what made them successful in the first place, and they end up losing their current loyal users. It may be that you no longer want to hang out with your old beer buddies as much as you did, and this may be a deliberate decision, but in most cases marketers only realize that they are alienating existing customers when they start seeing an exodus of erstwhile loyal users. The fiasco of the New Coke launch and its resulting alienation of existing users is staple fare for most marketing books, so I will not repeat that oft told tale. Instead, I will share some practical tips on how you can avoid such a mistake.

1. Know who your current loyal users are and why they are loyal to your brand. A hint is that for most brands, this is rarely just the functional benefit they offer, but also a combination of all the imagery, feelings and emotions they evoke. My favorite airline is Singapore Airlines, not just for the excellent connections and the amazing in-flight entertainment, but also due to the personalized service that makes entering a plane after a long trip something like a homecoming. If Singapore Airlines were to relaunch itself with a totally modernized fleet, improved in-flight amenities and better connections, none of that would ever compensate for the loss of the emotional connection if it slipped on its service.

2. Understand what makes your brand familiar and recognizable—what is your brand's "calling card"? This can be critical if you are thinking of changing the packaging, since you would ideally want to retain some elements of your brand-mark to help retain a bridge with your current

loyal consumers. There are several techniques to do this, but in essence it boils down to understanding which visual signals—shape, color, font or design element—come top of mind to consumers when they think of your brand. The great brands know this—Coke's red and white, Nike's swoosh and Marlboro's cowboy are all examples of how this understanding of the importance of having a consistent visual identity can go a long way in creating an enduring brand.

3. If you do relaunch, have a plan to talk to your current users so that they understand why you are changing and why they should stick with you. This communication could be in the form of a sticker on the new pack, an ad that shows what is better about your new product or service, or an offer that rewards loyal users to shift to your relaunch. In our earlier example, it may mean inviting the boys over for beer so you can explain what you are trying to do.

LESSON 20:
Substance over style—Offer something that really enhances the consumer experience, not cosmetic changes

I'm a jam freak, eating jam with toast pretty much every morning. As I was browsing the supermarket aisles yesterday and was about to reach for my usual brand, I was struck by the following words on a neighboring brand's pack: "Same great product, great new look." As a consumer I was left wondering why I would ever reconsider that brand just because their pack may look more esthetic, since the jam inside, by its own admission, is the same. To me that amounts to marketing suicide. Market experience shows what should be an obvious truth—that relaunches with purely cosmetic changes usually do not work as well as those that actually enhance the consumer experience in a meaningful way. I am not saying that you necessarily need to have an improved product to make a relaunch work, but it certainly does help. Even if you do not have a product or technological improvement to offer, you can make a relaunch a success if you ensure that you are offering your consumer some real improvement in what they get out of the total experience of your brand.

Think of all the points where consumers interact with your brand: when they see your ads, when they see your product in a store, when they are shelling out money to buy it, when they actually use it, and when they or others around them react to the impact that the brand has had on them. If your relaunch is not able to bring about a meaningful impact at one or more of these points of interaction between your consumers and your brand, you are unlikely to succeed. So become familiar with these points of contact, and then do a brutally honest assessment of whether the proposed changes to your brand do anything to really improve the consumer's experience at one or more of them.

In practical terms, you may find the following exercise useful when you are creating a relaunch or evaluating if the one you are working on is likely to succeed or not. List all the points of interaction, and then establish the current situation of how your brand fares on each of those as compared to your key competitors. For example, how does your product perform versus your competitors, how much do you spend on media compared to them, what do consumers feel about your packaging versus theirs, and so on. Then overlay your relaunch plans, and see if you are able to make a marked improvement on at least a couple of these factors versus where you are now. If you do not see such an improvement, then you have your work cut out for you.

As you can see, there is not one magic solution to creating a winning relaunch. Instead, there are many possible routes to success—better product experience, packaging that enhances the shopping experience through better sizing, pricing, information on the pack, a new proposition, etc. However, the point is to remember that the consumer does not buy your brand to frame the pretty packaging and hang it on the living room wall, so think beyond just cosmetic changes.

LESSON 21:
It takes more than one meeting to build a reputation—Don't move away too fast from a relaunch message

Assume your first meeting with your new clients was a big hit. You were able to impress them with your wit, and you did not really mind sipping wine and talking about golf. In fact, you think that they were far less stuffy than you had feared, and you would not mind meeting them again. However, chances are you may have made a good first impression, but it will not last unless you can carry it off every time you meet them.

It is the same with a relaunch—the initial relaunch may be strong, but often it will quickly run out of steam as consumers move on to the next big thing. In many relaunches, especially in consumer packaged goods, this is important since a relaunch brings with it a conversion on the shelf from the old product or pack to the new one. As a result, you may in fact lose distribution and trial, and unless you can get rapid and sustained trial and distribution built up, you could take several months just to return to where you used to be. The best relaunches are the ones that recognize the need for sustained support and plan for it proactively. The same principle applies for services as it does for products, as the basic dynamic of boosting awareness and trial holds true for them both.

If you are going to change some of the fundamentals that make your brand, whether it is your packaging or your proposition, never underestimate how long it can take to really get that message to sink in. What your brand stands for today probably took years to establish, so there is no reason to believe that in a matter of months, consumers will suddenly embrace and recognize the new you. Here are a couple of thoughts to help you sustain support on the relaunch and avoid consumers hopping from one message to another:

1. Just because you are bored with your advertising or message, do not assume that consumers are as well. As marketers, we live and breathe our brand's marketing every day, and it is easy to believe that something is "old" very soon. Set clear objectives on what kind of awareness and trial you want for your new message, and do not move until you see yourself hitting those numbers with consumers. In other words, your boredom does not count—listen to the consumer.

2. Plan for a second and third wave of marketing even before you relaunch. One way of thinking about this is to consider that despite your new message or proposition, you are unlikely to achieve 100% market share. There will always be consumers who will not convert to your brand. Learn what may hold them back and use that to plan for future waves of marketing, building on your relaunch message instead of jumping to another launch or project. In practical terms, this means doing the opposite of what most marketers do. Usually marketers spend a lot of time understanding what consumers find appealing in their brand, but to get this right, you will have to understand what consumers dislike about your offering. Go and talk to consumers who reject your proposition and understand what their barriers are, then plan for future waves of communication to bust these barriers. That is one proven way of ensuring that you do not move away from a relaunch message too soon.

When two's a crowd: Managing a portfolio of brands

O ne of the milestones in marketing history was the introduction of the concept of brand management in the 1930s. Simply put, each brand was to be treated as an independent business entity, competing externally as well as internally with other brands. This worked wonderfully until people realized that a more strategic approach was needed to manage a portfolio of brands. This realization was prompted by changing retail realities and by the increase in competitive clutter, when having your own brands trading users between each other did not grow total company sales. With the growth of large retailers and their greater bargaining power, the focus shifted from just growing a particular brand's sales to ideas that would grow the entire category. This change was driven by the recognition that retailers make more money only if the total pie grows, not just by shifting volumes from one brand to another. So "category management" became the new buzzword, and since then virtually every marketer has been walking the thin line between driving a brand as an independent unit and adjusting it for the greater good of the category. Whether you manage a portfolio of brands or simply want to learn more about how one should approach doing so, this is the chapter for you.

No stepping on each other's toes—Pull brands apart in the consumer's mind

As you start thinking about category management, the basic question you need to tackle is the best way of separating the brands in your portfolio so that they truly complement each other instead of just trading users and market share. One of the most common pitfalls is to automatically assume that a "clustering" of brands is best done based on features. This may be because as consumers ourselves, we often categorize products and brands by the features they have—for example, looking at horsepower as a way of grouping different classes of cars. That may be fine to start with, but as categories mature, consumers become more discerning. When this happens, the connections with a brand start going beyond its functional features, and as a result you will need to think about grouping brands by more than just what they do.

I would argue that the best way to have a differentiated portfolio of brands is to have clear and distinct target audiences for each. In other words, rather than differentiate based only on what the brands are, start with whom they want to target. This approach is as applicable for "technology driven" categories like cars and services like airlines as it is for fast-moving consumer goods. Airlines are a great example of this, where the demand for budget travel and competition from new budget competitors has led several airlines to launch "low cost" carriers supplementing their traditional carriers. One way of differentiating the two could be purely based on cost—in other words, strip out some features to enable the lower price. Doing so may make the numbers add up, but it would not necessarily delight the respective target audiences of each offering.

Another approach would be to start by considering what the target consumer—the budget traveler—would regard as unnecessary frills (e.g. Internet check-in, in-flight meals or movies on short flights) and then designing features based on this. The other big advantage of segmenting your brands based on who their target consumers are is that doing so often identifies new growth opportunities that would not be obvious if one focused solely on the brand's physical or functional features. In Lessons 13 to 15, we discussed the perils of extending a brand into multiple categories, but using a "consumer-centered" segmentation can yield powerful insights into where you could extend a brand, and also which brand in your portfolio would be best placed to extend into a new category.

LESSON 23:
I love you both, but... Be ruthless on the role each brand plays in your portfolio

Part of being a good marketer, and a good leader in general, is being decisive and making tough choices, and you will be tested on both when it comes to managing a portfolio of brands. What makes it harder is that in real-life marketing, you are dealing with real people whose lives and careers can be impacted by your decisions rather than with paper case studies. In the example above, the budget carrier would likely never get the same level of resources as the full-fare carrier, but both brands would have teams working on them who want to grow their respective businesses. It can be difficult to tell people that their brand will receive fewer resources or less support than another because of category priorities, but that is an example of the tough decisions that good category management entails.

Once the roles that different brands need to play are clear—ideally based on the segmentation of consumer needs, as discussed in Lesson 22—it is critical to follow this through with ruthlessness. The best of strategic differentiation can be undone if the strategic intent is forgotten in the course of everyday decision-making.

In the airline example, one of the choices to be made would probably be that advances in technology (the latest planes, the more comfortable seats, the better in-flight entertainment systems, etc.) would ideally go first to the full-fare carrier before possibly filtering down to the budget carrier. If the airline did not do this, there is little reason you could expect consumers to pay more for the premium carrier. Brand managers on the budget carrier, interested primarily in growing their brand's sales, could be forgiven for making demands that the better seats and entertainment systems be installed on their planes at the same time. However, the real test of category management comes in staying true to the role each brand is to play in the portfolio—maximizing the sum of both brands, even if it means each brand individually may be constrained in some way.

That is not to say that you should play favorites in any way or set up one brand for failure. You still want each brand to stay true to the principles of classical brand management and remain focused on growing its business as an entrepreneurial unit. Where category management would add value is in helping the brands stay true to their roles in the portfolio so they can win with the business model that is right for their assigned role. In the airline example, even if you felt like being generous and told the budget carrier that it could install the new and more expensive seats or entertainment systems, this may in fact be a handicap and prevent it from best playing its role in the portfolio. This is because the increased cost would put pressure on its ability to be priced competitively versus other budget carriers, which was the reason for its existence in the first place.

LESSON 24:
The wonder of scale—Use the portfolio to your advantage

Any financial advisor worth his salt will tell you that the secret to wealth generation is diversification, so that losses in any one area can be compensated for by gains in another area. In plain English, it is better not to put all your eggs in one basket. This is also the beauty of having a portfolio of brands—ups and downs are inevitable on any brand, but with a portfolio of brands, chances are high that one could be used to compensate for weakness in another and buy you time while you fix the problem brand. You can take this a step further by using a portfolio of brands strategically—the key is to have a strategic game plan. If you focus on trying to maximize each brand in isolation, you will miss out on one of the biggest advantages of having a portfolio: scale.

At it broadest level, you can use the portfolio to balance out top and bottom line growth. If you need to invest disproportionately in one brand for top line growth—for example, to launch in a new market or segment where you may not make much money in the short term—you can compensate by pricing actions or cost savings in another brand to meet profitability. When it comes to winning in stores, piggybacking one brand on another, especially if the second is stronger or more widely distributed, and using pooled funds for joint displays are examples of the benefits of having a portfolio to work with. Having a portfolio of brands working well for you can also be a big source of competitive advantage. If competition heats up, you could choose to use one of your brands to do tactical promotions or activities versus scrambling to make changes on all of your brands.

In air warfare, the concept of a "wingman" is widely used, where pilots fly in pairs and the wingman is assigned to make sure the other plane can complete its mission and is protected from enemy attack. With a portfolio of brands, you can use individual brands to work as a wingman for others, fending off competitive attack. In the Indian Cola Wars of the 1990s, both Coke and Pepsi entered the country at about the same time, sparking off a vicious battle for market share. Pepsi was at its usual irreverent best, but rather than use the flagship Coke brand to respond, Coca-Cola used a strong local brand it had acquired, Thums Up, to take on a more youthful positioning and do a lot of "in your face" tactical advertising and promotions against Pepsi. Doing so allowed the company to stay the course on building awareness and equity for Coke. In doing so, Coke successfully leveraged the strength of its portfolio instead of relying solely on one brand to fight its battles.

This brings to a close the first "P" of marketing that we took on— positioning. By now, I hope I have been able to give you a taste of the real decisions a marketer faces in positioning a brand and setting it up for success. But a marketer's task does not end there. You may have the best mousetrap in the world, but you will not sell a single one unless your potential buyers know what you have. That brings us to the second "P" we will tackle in this book—promotion.

PROMOTION

*In the modern world of business, it is useless to be
a creative original thinker unless you can also sell
what you create.*

- David Ogilvy

A strong positioning for your brand counts for very little unless you can communicate it to your consumers. It is tempting to assume that promotion is essentially about making the right media choices, and indeed a lot of textbooks go into this with a fair bit of detail. However, in the real-world marketplace, promotion is much more complex than just figuring out your media plan. It is marketing at its best: part art, when it comes to transforming your strategic positioning to advertising and promotional materials that bring it to life; and part science, in terms of making the right spending and media choices.

In the real world, your messages are not reaching the consumer in a vacuum, but rather are competing for both media and mind space with your competition. Also, in recent years the use of media beyond "traditional" TV-centric models has been part of the staple diet of marketing literature. While it is impossible to discuss each and every media choice, this section will give you some tips on how to choose between some of the different vehicles available for reaching your consumer.

What starts well ends well: The importance of a good brief

Whether it is a multimillion-dollar advertising campaign you are embarking upon, or just deciding what to put on the poster for your small business, there is one common factor that determines the success of your promotional campaign. It is the clarity of the brief with which a project begins. Whether you are working with an advertising agency or you are going to develop the material yourself, before jumping into execution it is critical to step back and be clear about what you are trying to achieve.

LESSON 25:
The power of one—Learn to be single-minded

The biggest factor that makes life difficult for advertisers is that usually the intended recipient is not actively seeking out their ads. So the burden of communication rests largely with the advertiser. Given the huge amount of communication we are all exposed to everyday, this makes it difficult for any ad to break through the clutter and register with consumers. Great execution aside, what usually marks out an ad's ability to do so is single-mindedness.

Let's take a simple test. Try to recall three ads you have seen or heard in the last 24 hours. Now, try to remember the key message in each ad. Difficult, isn't it? Thinking like a consumer is a sobering experience for most marketers as it teaches the humbling truth that there is more to consumers' lives than watching ads. So why not make everyone's life simpler by giving consumers a single, simple message to remember instead of a litany of all the things your brand can do. A lot of ads I see seem like an internal company memo, listing a whole bunch of features or benefits but lacking one message I can hang on to. At the end of it all, the consumer is left with little more to remember than the brand being advertised, if that.

A simple tip is to avoid asking the question, "What do I want to communicate to the consumer?" before you start a promotional campaign, because chances are that you want to say a whole lot, much of which will not register anyway. Instead, reframe the question as, "What is the one thing I want consumers to take away from my communication?" That one thing could be determined by which message you feel (or even better, which message your consumer research tells you) is the one that makes consumers desire your offering, or the one message that best encapsulates what you want your brand to stand for in the consumer's mind.

Here is an example that brings some of these principles to life in a very personal context—that of looking for a job. Imagine you are trying to "advertise" yourself to a potential employer through your resume for a position that requires leading a large team. As a well educated and talented young person, you probably have a lot of skills and experiences you could bring to the table. However, knowing that leadership of large teams is the core skill this employer is looking for, what is the one thing you would want your cover letter to shout out—your experience in leading large teams, or all sorts of other things like your analytical skills, your willingness to travel and your knowledge of word processing? Simple answer, isn't it? Why should marketing be any more complicated?

LESSON 26:
Good things come to those who wait—Be patient

A good friend of mine who worked as a freelance producer of advertising once taught me an invaluable lesson about advertising. One evening, he told me about an unreasonable client who seemed to demand great results on short timelines, but was unwilling to pay the amount of money that would be needed to deliver on his requirements. In between curses and swigs of beer, he said something every marketer should know: "Cheap, fast and good—you can only have two at a time, the other will have to give."

Ten years and more than a hundred ads later, I realize just how true those words are, and just how critical it is to remember them when you set out to create any promotional campaign. Try it yourself: imagine you want a promotional campaign with great quality but you have only a modest budget at your disposal. If you really want it to happen, chances are that you need to be prepared to be patient as you or your agency find the best suppliers, plan out timings, search for the right models and in general look for ideas on how you could cut costs while not compromising on quality. The bottom line is that getting exceptional quality requires either enough money to make it happen or enough time to get the quality you want at a reasonable cost.

If you are indeed in a hurry, a position in which marketers sometimes find themselves—whether it is because they need to meet the timing of a launch, are reacting to a competitive threat or just responding to unreasonable demands from their boss—know that one of the other two (cost or quality) will usually give. If you are faced with such a situation, the best thing to do is to be clear on what you are willing to trade off. As with many aspects of marketing, there is no easy right or wrong answer; instead, it is all about making choices with your eyes wide open. This lesson does not offer much by way of solutions, but it does highlight the sobering reality that every marketer should know to avoid setting unrealistic expectations of themselves and their agencies or suppliers.

LESSON 21:
Who is going along on the journey? Be clear on who is part of the process

Everyone has a point of view on advertising. Many people who would keep absolutely mum when a scientist is talking about the features of a new product or an accountant is holding forth about details of taxation planning will be very vocal in offering free advice on advertising—whether it be the selection of models, the storyline in the ad or the choice of music. I think this is due to two reasons. First, as consumers or viewers, we are the recipients of so much advertising that it becomes almost a part of popular culture like movies or sports. As a result, it tends to become something on which everyone finds it only natural to have an opinion. Second, advertising is nowhere near as exact a science as, say, engineering or medicine, and so people assume that it is something anyone can do.

While advertising is certainly not a science, there is something to be said for training and experience. Going back to the analogy I used in the introduction, a lot of people watch martial arts movies, and almost every kid thinks he knows some moves. Put one of these armchair Bruce Lees in the ring against someone who has actually trained for years, and the difference between an interested amateur and a trained specialist would be brutally obvious. If you are a marketer, you need to think of yourself that way, and be clear about who the other "specialists" are on your team as you create a great campaign—be they fellow marketers, your agency, or your suppliers. Inevitably, there will always be the interested amateurs who will offer free advice—senior management, the sales director, your secretary, your spouse and pretty much anyone else who knows you work in marketing—but it is up to you to draw a clear line regarding who has a say in the work.

One of the keys to success is the ability to filter out this background noise and work toward excellence in strategy and execution with your colleagues, confident in the knowledge that you know your brand and consumer, and are more than an interested amateur when it comes to advertising. That takes guts, especially when it comes to dealing with gratuitous advice on what to do with your advertising, and lessons on what makes for great advertising. The former I cannot transmit through a book. For the latter, read on and get started.

What if you were dating your viewer? How to develop great TV advertising

I cringe every time someone refers to TV advertising as a "mass medium." It makes it sound so sterile and impersonal that it is not surprising that so much of the advertising out there comes across as cold and impersonal, like a memo to the consumer explaining what benefits the brand offers instead of actually striving to make a lasting connection with the consumer. I like to think of it differently. To me, there is nothing "mass" about TV advertising—every time a consumer sees your ad, it is a one-on-one interaction, and a chance for you to make a lasting connection. To help you see what that kind of thinking may lead you to do, let us change the context to one that is all about making a one-on-one connection: dating.

Making truly great TV advertising—ads that do not just sell your product but also begin to resonate in the consumer's heart and mind—is a lot like dating. If you have ever courted or been courted by someone, I imagine you already know, perhaps without realizing it, some tricks to develop such advertising—tricks that no business school would teach you.

Appearances count! Learn the power of visualization

At the risk of sounding politically incorrect, how a person looks has a lot to do with how we feel about him or her. I hear you saying that it is what's inside that really matters, and thinking of appearances alone sounds pretty shallow. I am not talking about whether a person looks "beautiful" or not, but how he or she presents himself or herself. Let's face it—if you bumped into two people of the opposite sex, one who looked well groomed and another who looked shabby and unkempt, who would you likely talk to first? Making a favorable visual first impression is a proven way to get beyond the first step and then onto really getting to know each other. That is because how you present yourself says a lot about you—how well you can take care of yourself, how well off you are and so on.

It is a similar story with TV advertising, since it is even more of a visual medium than dating. One of the most common errors I have seen in TV advertising is the tendency to agonize over the words to be used while giving the visuals very little attention. Once again, you must recognize that the consumer's life has more facets than simply seeking out information about your product. With a consumer who is busy arguing with the spouse, handling bratty kids, flipping channels, thinking about work deadlines and doing a hundred other things at once, the best chance you have of getting the consumer's attention is to present a simple yet powerful visualization of what your brand offers. The old cliché of a picture being worth a thousand words is indeed very true when it comes to developing TV advertising that works.

If we go back to Lesson 25, we saw the importance of being selective about what you want to communicate. This lesson is about creating the best single visual or set of visuals that brings your chosen message to life in a way that grabs the consumer's attention amidst the clutter of ads that fly past them every day. Some practical tips to make this happen:

1. Before you see a single frame of the storyboard or hear the brilliant copy that will blow the consumer away, demand to first see a single visual that brings your chosen proposition to life. This will force your agency to give this the importance it deserves in the advertising development process.

2. Imagine that this is the only visual you have to sell your brand, and evaluate whether it (1) stays true to the benefit you have chosen to hang your hat on, (2) is distinctive versus what other brands have

in their advertising, and (3) is simple enough to understand in one glance.

3. Demand that this visual comes across at every opportunity the consumer has to interact with your brand, including your TV advertising, in-store materials, print advertising and so on. This will not only ensure that you have a strong visual to communicate what your brand stands for, but also that it is something your consumers will see with consistency no matter where your brand's message happens to reach them.

LESSON 29:
Nobody dates a bore—Engage, don't ramble on about yourself

I once knew a guy who loved talking about himself. Every time I bumped into him, I would hear all about his latest trips abroad, his latest fancy gadget, his misguided attempts to become sophisticated by learning golf, and, of course, his lack of success in his love life. The last would not have been a surprise to him if he knew just how boring it was to sit and passively listen to all he had to say about himself. The sure way to end a budding relationship is to fall into this "bore trap." Conversely, a sure fire way to get a relationship off to a great start is to be interesting company. No prizes for guessing how important this is in TV advertising as well.

The "bore trap" in advertising is evident when the ad is a 30-second monologue from the manufacturer about all that the brand has to offer. Once again, marketing becomes easier if you can learn to think of yourself as a consumer. Now for another quick quiz:

1. Which ad do you remember bringing a smile to your face?
2. Is there a jingle or tune from an ad that you hummed long after you saw the ad?
3. Is there an ad you and your friends discussed after seeing?

These ads were probably memorable because they piqued your interest through engaging drama, humor, music or storytelling. Don't get me wrong—I am not advocating "interesting" ads that do not sell the product. Advertising is not making a video for art's sake, but rather it is a commercial endeavor that hinges on selling the advertised product or service. Great advertising does not just sell the product, but it also makes the brand stick in the consumer's mind and heart. It goes beyond just advertising the proposition offered, using engaging drama, storytelling and sound design to create an unforgettable impression.

I hear you saying, "But I don't do all of that, the agency does, so what role do I play in this?" You hit the nail on the head—your main role is to liberate your agency to deliver great execution, after equipping them with a clear and single-minded strategy. Too many marketers act like frustrated creatives, juggling frames on a storyboard and giving their own "value-added" comments on the storytelling, instead of focusing on where they can really add value—ensuring that the creative output delivers on the strategic proposition, and then fully using the advertising agency's talents to elevate the message to great advertising.

In a real-life date, you would not normally have back-up telling you what to do and what not to, but in courting your consumer, you do have someone whispering the right words to say in your ears—your agency.

LESSON 30:
The power of "ummm"—Empathize with strong insights

When I was single, I would wonder what makes some people decide that they have found the person just right for them. Now, happily married, I think it has a lot to do with finding someone who really seems to understand you and with whom you are able to share everything that is on your mind, without fear of being judged. That is the power of empathy. One of the ways to deliver great TV advertising, and advertising in general, is to harness this powerful emotion.

What does this mean? Imagine your consumers are sitting across the table from you. What would you do to show that you empathize with them? My list would include some common sense tips like not passing judgment on them too hastily; showing that I am genuinely interested in listening to them; not putting them down in any way; and showing that while I may not necessarily be like them, I am willing to make a genuine attempt to understand where they are coming from. Sounds simple, right? Why does advertising have to be any more difficult? It is just a shift of mindset, from thinking of advertising as some arcane skill taught in business schools or by pony-tailed gurus, to thinking of it as the systematic application of some basic skills we all possess, such as the ability to connect with others.

Here are some practical tips on applying these thoughts to advertising:

1. Do not assume your consumer is like you or the people you hang out with. When you hear that your brand's advertising does not "connect," a good place to start looking is to check whether the marketing team is developing communication for itself or for its consumers. I heard a story once about a marketer who was observing a focus group, and while fiddling with her Prada bag, scoffed at the consumers seated on the other side of the one-way mirror and wondered why they weren't more "beautiful." Recognize, respect and remember who your consumers are as individuals—no matter how different they may be from you.

2. If you want to understand someone, there is no substitute for walking a mile in his shoes. Meet your consumers, visit their homes, meet their families, go shopping with them, and you may begin to understand a bit of what makes them tick. You will never get that kind of understanding from reading any number of research reports or crunching consumer data on your computer.

3. Know the broader issues in your consumer's life beyond just the benefit area your brand is selling. Doing so may allow you to make connections that extend far beyond the functional benefit your brand has to offer. The trend toward environmental consciousness, for example, has spawned a growing market for a host of "natural" products, while the stresses of modern living have made the "self help" industry boom. Make the effort to know what bothers your consumers in their day-to-day lives and you may well enable your brand to ride on the next big trend.

Testing, testing, 1, 2, 3: Using advertising testing smartly

Everyone tests advertising, from the multinational paying thousands of dollars for large-scale quantitative research to the small businessman running his promotional flyer by his wife before he prints it. The methods may vary widely, but the underlying motivation is very similar—before you put out something that could have a huge impact on your business' short-term fortunes, you want to make sure that you are not screwing up. And as with most fields of human endeavor, where there is a need, there are those offering solutions for the right price. As a result, advertising testing has become a booming industry, with various proprietary techniques available to test whether an ad will deliver added sales and communicate the desired message. It is not my intent to talk about these in any detail, but rather to share some principles for you to keep in mind, no matter how you end up testing your advertising.

Do you do research before falling in love? Learn to use and develop your instincts

I love the process of creating advertising, as it brings to life all that I love about marketing—winning with creativity and big ideas, translating consumer insight into action, and seeing your efforts play out in the real world. Advertising testing has several benefits, as it enables you to assess how well your advertising is likely to do, and it brings in some science to help structure the art associated with the process of creating advertising. However, the problem with too much testing is that it takes something that should be creative and turns it into a sterile, academic exercise. That is the first pitfall to avoid if you embark on advertising testing.

Think back to when you last fell in love. Did you carefully tabulate data on the person you had in mind, weigh the pros and cons, and then decide whether or not to take the plunge? More likely than not, your story may have been like mine, when the realization that I had met that special someone just hit me like a bolt of lightning. You can call it instinct or a gut feeling, but what it was certainly not was an intellectual decision. Where am I going with this? Simply to the point that if I can decide on the person who I am going to spend the rest of my life with based on gut instinct, I'll be damned if the decision of whether to air an ad for the next six months becomes an agonizing, data-churning, intellectual exercise.

Don't get me wrong—testing is invaluable as a risk management and diagnostic tool. It is a great way of knowing how good your chances are of building business, and whether your message is hitting the right mark. But it is not a substitute for judgment. What you need to do is gain some experience so that you can hone your ability to make more gut-based decisions. So learn all about how your ads and those of your competition test, learn what works and what does not, and then use this knowledge to sharpen your gut instinct so that when you see an idea, storyboard or script, you react with your gut rather than going into an intellectual spiral of blindly testing and testing again. Once in a while, if you really believe in an ad, take the leap of faith and go with it without testing. You will learn heaps, your agency will respect you, and you will certainly have more fun. It takes patience, time and courage to develop your instincts to their full potential, but who said that falling in love was risk-free?

Lasting love or a forgettable first date? Ensure that you are memorable

How many times has someone of the opposite sex crossed your path and really turned your head—whether it was because of looks, personality or something else? Unless you are a monk or a saint, I am guessing several times at least. And unless you have accumulated a harem of everyone who has ever struck your fancy, I am guessing that you decided on one person as your partner or spouse. What set that person apart? What makes the difference between a lasting relationship and a passing fancy? It may be many things—circumstances, timing, or intangible things like making a connection—but at the core is the residual impact this person had on you. In other words, the simple fact that he or she somehow "stuck" in your mind long after you first met.

In advertising, the ability to stand out and make a consumer choose your brand depends to a large extent on residual impact. Simply put, do people remember your message after they have been exposed to it? This is critical because this residual impact then kicks in and influences the consumer's decision when it is time to choose a brand. The decision typically occurs long after the ad was seen, whether it takes place while browsing the shelves in the supermarket or clicking a "Buy" button on the Internet. So if you really want to see how good your ad is, don't just go by what people say when they are exposed to it—check for whether they remember it at all, and what they remember about it a day or two later. That is a tougher test and a more realistic measure of whether your ad is likely to affect purchase decision than any instant feedback you get, no matter how positive it may be.

Unfortunately, most people will often not remember exactly what your ad said, and a lot of them won't remember seeing it at all. But if you can overcome the obstacles and connect with your consumer in a way that makes them remember your message, it will be the difference between a 30-second flirtation with your consumer and creating a lasting relationship.

Would she leave her boyfriend for you? Don't just measure appeal, measure conversion

It seems fashionable nowadays to talk of "win-win" solutions. When it comes to marketing, this is usually a fallacy for the simple reason that in most markets and categories, winning over a consumer or a share point means it has to come at the expense of a competitor. The failure to recognize and plan for this simple reality is a major reason why advertising that otherwise seems brilliant sometimes fails to deliver.

I had a friend in college who was head over heels in love with a girl we both knew. They were pretty good friends and shared similar interests, and it seemed that all he had to do was to work up the courage to propose. One evening, he did, and received an answer for which he was not prepared. She told him that he was a good friend and she really liked him, but she already had a boyfriend—she had been in a long-distance relationship for more than a year, and she could not leave him.

You are probably not interested in my friend's love life, but this is exactly what happens every day when what you thought was the irresistible force of your advertising bumps into the consumers' immovable loyalty to their current brand. If despite all your great marketing you are unable to achieve the share or sales growth you wanted, one reason could be that your consumers are telling you that they like you just fine, but they are too committed to their current brand to bother switching to you.

Part of this could be due to a real loyalty forged by great marketing on the part of the consumer's chosen brand, but often a key role is played by simple inertia—why change from something that is proven to work and risk trying something new? Here are some simple practical tips you could use to make sure you are giving the right reasons why your consumer should switch to you:

1. As you start designing your message, spend the time to understand competitive users: How loyal are they? What creates this loyalty? Are there any weaknesses that you could exploit? Is there a segment of current users who are less loyal than the rest?

2. Once you have your message crafted and are ready to test it, do not just test whether consumers like it, but also test the extent to which it is likely to make them shift from their current brand.

3. If converting competitive users is critical, try to replicate the real marketplace as much as possible. Test your messages side by side

with the competitors' and then see which of your messages brings about the most shift in preference to your brand.

You will never be able to fully replicate the real-world marketplace in any research you do, but the above may help you bridge the gap between theory and reality to some extent. Doing so will improve your ability to predict how your advertising will fare when it comes head-to-head against what your competition has in store for you.

Radio gaga: Developing radio advertising

Long before humans began writing things down or bringing ideas to life through pictures, they were telling stories. Some of mankind's oldest epics began as oral traditions, and they continued that way for centuries before they were ever put down on paper. That tradition continues to an extent today as well. Some of my earliest childhood memories are of my father telling me stories at night, conjuring up fantastic tales of demons, monsters and heroes, tales so real that I could almost see them unfold before my eyes. So, what does this have to do with marketing?

Imagine that you cannot show a single picture or written word to your consumer.

Imagine that you have less than a minute to convince them to choose your brand.

Welcome to the wonderful world of radio advertising! Radio is not as much in vogue today as it once was as an advertising medium, but it still does find its takers. The reason I am devoting a chapter to it is not because of its relative importance as a medium, but because radio throws up some unique and fascinating challenges for the marketer, which can teach you a lot about marketing communication in general.

Can you "see" your radio ad? Use visualization to create great radio spots

Like many people, I am not a great fan of movie adaptations of books. This is because a lot of people, myself included, like to visualize books. When I am really into a book, I may not remember exact phrases or words, but I tend to remember the story visually, creating images of scenes and characters that stay with me. When I think of the book later, it is almost like remembering something that I saw unfold before me in real life or on a movie screen, rather than something that I read on paper. That is the magic of a great book, and to top it requires great movie making. Long before J.R.R. Tolkien's creations were brought to life by Peter Jackson, I could have told you what I thought Frodo looked like, and how Gollum may have grinned looking at the Ring. That is the kind of magic you need to create truly great radio advertising, since by the very nature of the medium, you cannot put any visual stimuli in front of your consumer.

When approaching radio advertising, marketers tend to evaluate "scripts," looking for the "right" words to communicate what they want. As a result, a lot of energy goes into choosing words and phrases that by themselves may summarize your message, but may not be quite enough to enable the consumer to visualize what you are offering. I would recommend a simple but very different approach to evaluating radio advertising. Ask your agency to read out the ad to you. As you hear the words, close your eyes and imagine what you "see," "hear" and "feel." If the spot is for coffee and you cannot conjure up what it must "smell" like or "taste" the brew being advertised, chances are you may be saying all the right words, but not really creating the kind of impact that will stay with the consumer.

Part of the trick in doing this well lies in setting the right expectations for your agency. Demand radio advertising that goes beyond a summary of your proposition and that leaves a lasting visual impression on your consumer. Some ways of doing this include using engaging storytelling, creating memorable characters or taking the time to set the stage for the context in which your proposition is being advertised, instead of rushing to list a litany of what your brand offers. Radio as a medium is about much more than the words in your script. The next lesson will offer hints on how to harness the elements of this medium.

LESSON 35:
The sound of silence—Use sound design, not just words

The unique challenge of radio advertising is one of its most fascinating opportunities—the absence of any visual stimuli. As a result, you have to rely solely on what the listener can hear. In trying to work around this, let us seek inspiration from music.

What is your favorite band? I listen to all kinds of music, and my iPod has a pretty eclectic mix—from Limp Bizkit to Aerosmith and Cat Stevens to Coldplay. What is it that you like about your favorite music? For me, it is a combination of things. In several cases the lyrics really strike a chord with me (think Living on the Edge or Father and Son). In other cases, it is the way that the music really sets the tone for the kind of mood I am in. I would venture that the same principles hold for great radio advertising. Think of your radio ad not as an opportunity to cram as much information as you can into a few seconds of communication, but as creating a piece of entertainment that your listener would want on his or her playlist. I am not advocating that you turn your brand into a music label, but rather that you understand and harness the power of sound design.

Sound design means the total listening experience you are able to create using music, special effects, words, and yes, sometimes silence. If you want to conjure up images of the power of your bike, how about using the sound of it revving to life? If you want to get someone thinking about your soft drink, how about the sound of the can popping open and the fizz of the drink pouring into a glass? Want to get someone thinking about buying Valentine's Day cards? Nothing beats soft, romantic music. While a picture may be worth a thousand words, when it comes to radio advertising, a sound is worth a whole lot more. Effective sound design can be very powerful. The simple way of going about it is not to stop at the script or the words when you evaluate radio advertising. Ask yourself and your agency, "What will be the total listening experience for the consumer?" Then force yourself to think beyond just the words and look instead at all the tricks of the trade you could use—music, sound effects, pauses at the right moments, the right inflection and emphasis, and so on. It is much more fun than looking at words typed on a piece of paper, and it could transform your spot into something you and your consumer will love.

LESSON 36:

Haven't I heard that before? Tailor for the medium; don't just repeat your TV ad

Do you like giving cards to your loved ones? I make it a point to give my wife a card every month on the day we were married. It is not the card *per se* that matters, but it just gives me an opportunity to let her know how much she means to me. Suppose a special day for a loved one is coming up (say an anniversary or a birthday), and you want to give the person a card saying how much you value the relationship. Sounds like a plan, right? Now imagine that you want to go beyond just a card and do something different with some old-fashioned charm. You sit down and write a letter. How romantic.

Now imagine the horror when the card is opened to reveal that the card and the letter have exactly the same words! Most of the brownie points you were hoping to score would likely dissipate pretty quickly. I can see you raising your eyebrows and saying something to the effect of, "What kind of idiot would do something like that?" The short answer is that most marketers would. What seems like common sense in an everyday context is a trap that a lot of marketers fall into when approaching radio advertising (or advertising on any media other than TV). That is the trap of repeating exactly the same message across the different media that the consumer may be exposed to. There is a situation where using different media to communicate the same message helps—when the added medium is helping you reach new users whom your TV ads may not be reaching. In our example above, this would mean giving your card and your letter to different people.

However, in cases where the various media are working together to reach your consumers in different contexts, such as TV and radio, force yourself to ask what unique spin you could put on your message to fully use the unique opportunities of each medium. At the end of the day, radio does have its limitations versus TV advertising, simply due to the lack of any visuals. So if you do choose to use radio, be clear on what aspect of your message you want to drive—ideally one that does not require visuals as a critical part of the communication. Radio is great as a reminder or a call to action (e.g. asking viewers to enter a contest or promotion), as it is in driving recall of some core elements of your message that require sound design (e.g. signature music or a jingle), but blindly repeating what your TV ad said will likely lead to nothing more than wasted media money.

Sex appeal sells, but what? Using celebrity advertising smartly

When I see how much celebrities earn from their advertising contracts, I often wonder if the amount of money paid is a reflection of their contribution to building a brand. If that were the case, then marketers must be quite useless, since many top celebrities earn for a few days of shooting what the entire marketing team on the brand would earn in a year! Using celebrities in advertising somehow conjures up all the glamorous things we associate with advertising, but if you want to learn how to smartly use celebrities to build your brand, I have some bad news for you.

As a marketer, you need to think of the decision to use a celebrity with the same detachment you would any other marketing decision, asking yourself the simple question of whether using a celebrity would help you create more sales or build your brand's equity. In many instances, the answer is no, so instead of jumping on the bandwagon because everyone seems to be using one, go spend your marketing money elsewhere. But in case you are convinced that using a celebrity may be right for your brand, read on.

Popularity isn't everything—Find a celebrity who fits your brand

When a brand has decided to use a celebrity, quite often the mindset seems to be, "Let's go find the biggest celebrity we can afford." That is not just simplistic, but also potentially dangerous. This kind of thinking sounds good in internal memos and may excite the sales force, but in reality, using a celebrity to build a brand may be downright silly. That is because the celebrity you choose to represent your brand is not just a pretty face to put on TV or plaster stores with, but instead is someone who comes to embody your brand for many consumers. As a result, the choice of a celebrity should be a strategic decision, taken with a full understanding of what such a choice could mean for your brand's equity and perception among consumers, not a tactical decision based on signing up the latest pin-up favorite.

There is no real science to it, but here are two questions to ask:

1. What is the marketing task you are trying to achieve by using a celebrity? If you find yourself mumbling something about "creating buzz," go bungee jumping to get your excitement instead of wasting your brand's scarce marketing dollars. My rule of thumb is to use a celebrity for three different reasons, and each task lends itself to a certain kind of celebrity. A celebrity can be used to: (1) break out of the clutter to get faster awareness and trial, (2) enhance the believability or credibility of your brand, and (3) increase your brand's equity through equity rub-off from the celebrity. In the first case, you may well get away with using a familiar face, but if you want to do either of the other two, you need to go beyond familiarity. For the second objective, you need to understand which celebrity would be a credible endorser for your brand, and for the third you need to look at a character fit between the brand and the celebrity, which brings me to the second question.

2. What is the brand character of your brand and does your celebrity embody it? Marketers have long used the concept of brand character, or brand personality, as a way of defining and differentiating brands. Simply put, it refers to the values, attitudes and character traits you would expect your brand to embody if it were a person. So if you are choosing a celebrity, certainly look at popularity, but also ask yourself if that celebrity could embody what you want your brand to stand for. As an extreme example, a family health brand

like Lifebuoy or Safeguard would probably face equity suicide if it used a young, sexy celebrity known for sleeping around with every second co-star.

LESSON 38:
Remember who pays your salary! Sell your brand, not the celebrity

The problem with top celebrities is that they can command a lot of money, and they know it only too well. As a result, some celebrities seem to appear in every second ad you see on TV, from biscuits to alcohol, and quite often, they all pass by in a blur. And all that is left in the viewer's mind is that it was yet another ad for the celebrity, with little recall of the brand that was actually being advertised or what that brand was offering. This is what I call "celebrity hijacking"—when in their excitement at having signed up a celebrity and in their desire to extract every last benefit they can get out of their deal, marketers sacrifice their basic brand communication in favor of showcasing the celebrity. It is a great way of further raising the "market value" of the celebrity, but not usually one of building your brand. I am not saying that you should pay oodles of money for a top celebrity and then waste the opportunity by having him appear in only one obscure scene in your ad. The key is to strike a balance between fully exploiting all the advantages a celebrity can bring to your brand, while ensuring that your ad remains focused on selling your brand, not the celebrity.

A practical tip to protect your advertising from being hijacked is to do the following exercise:

1. Write down the top three things that you want consumers to take away from your advertising. A simple way to do this is to imagine that the consumers who have just watched your ad are sitting in front of you. If you asked them what they remember about the ad, what would be your dream answer? Chances are that you would like the consumers to recall the brand being advertised, as well as remembering something about the proposition you are offering and some of the elements of your storytelling, such as the use of the celebrity.

2. Force yourself to put the celebrity endorsement as the last priority and put the top two as things relating to your brand's strategic message and branding.

3. When you see your communication material or test it among consumers, make sure the top two objectives are coming out stronger

than the celebrity endorsement—in simple terms, are consumers recalling your core message more than the fact that you have a well-known face in your ad?

True love or a one-ad stand? Build brand ambassadors, not just paid models

Let's assume that you have a celebrity who fits perfectly with your brand and you have learned to use him in a way that builds your brand's image. The worst thing you could do now is to treat him like any other model who acts in your advertising. There are a couple of reasons for this. The first is a pragmatic one relating to the fact that celebrities tend to be highly visible in media, and your advertising will likely not be the only place your consumer sees and hears them talking about your brand. A nightmare scenario would be to pay top dollar for a great ad with a celebrity and then have the celebrity say in an interview that he personally uses another brand! The second reason for not treating your celebrity like just another model is that if you really want to build credibility or an equity rub-off, the relationship between your brand and the celebrity needs to go beyond one ad or one year. Ideally you want to create a long-term association, since these things take time and repeated exposure to build. The following are some thoughts on how you can create a lasting relationship with your celebrity:

1. Get them to really believe in your brand. Send them your products or get them to experience your service, and make sure that they would personally advocate it before you put them in an ad. Encourage them to use their own mannerisms and language in talking about your brand instead of handing them a script to read out—you will be amazed at the difference that can make between a celebrity appearing as a paid model versus a passionate advocate of your brand.

2. Use them for more than just paid advertising—use a good public relations agency or your own resources to arrange interviews or features highlighting why they endorse your brand. These appearances will likely help build more credibility about their endorsement than any number of branded TV spots ever would.

3. Learn to manage them the way they like to be managed—via a single point of contact, preferably at a relatively senior level, and with some personal touch. Celebrities are only human and respond better to

relationships than just material incentives. So the worst thing you can do is to have a different person call on them every time. Find someone who knows the business (could be someone in your agency as well) and is experienced at relationship management, and make them the "face" of your brand for the celebrity and their managers.

Getting down and dirty: The risky business of competitive advertising

I suspect that there are a lot of armchair generals tucked away in the cubicles and conference rooms of the marketing departments of companies. That is perhaps why military analogies resonate so well with marketers—we talk of launching new campaigns, of attacking competitive strongholds, of defending against attack, and of capturing market share. These analogies yield a lot of interesting insights, and are great for rallying the troops and for injecting some excitement into work.

The strength of your advertising gets tested when you find yourself face-to-face with the "enemy."

There are many reasons people become overtly competitive in their advertising. You may be trying to exploit some weakness in your competitor's product, you may be trying to respond to claims it has made, or you may just be trying to attract its users by telling them how your brand is better. Whatever the reason, this is one area where I recommend throwing simplistic military analogies out the window. If you want to embark upon the risky business of becoming really competitive in your advertising, put aside clichés of "smashing the enemy" or "launching decapitating strikes" (both phrases I have heard people use) and read on.

Pissing contests never built brands—Speak to your consumer, not your competitor

What would you do if someone walked up to you in the street and slapped you? If you were the next Mahatma Gandhi, you may well offer the other cheek, but I'm guessing you would react angrily like most ordinary mortals. I also imagine you would have a strong urge to retaliate. There is nothing wrong with that—it is a perfectly normal instinct to defend ourselves when attacked. The problem is when you take that instinct into business decisions. In today's intensely competitive markets, an ad disparaging your brand or copying your claims can feel just as personal an affront as a slap on the face. It is thus perfectly understandable why a lot of advertising out there looks more like brand managers trading slaps over the airwaves than trying to communicate anything to the consumer. However, when it comes to competitive advertising, such a knee-jerk response may not really do anything for your brand.

I lay no claims to being a saint, so while I feel it is a waste of marketing money to start an all-out battle with a competitor, there are occasions when you will have to engage in fairly blatant competitive advertising. At the top of my list of those occasions is when you find competition making false claims disparaging your brand. A close second is when you have a clear advantage over your competitive brand that you can exploit. The only caveat is to remember that the target for your advertising is your consumer, not your competitor. So, before you put anything in your ad that is remotely competitive, ask yourself one simple question: how does this make a difference to your consumer?

As an example, suppose you have found an area where your product or service is better than your competition. Instead of just hammering that point across to rub your competitor's nose in it, ask yourself how that advantage makes your consumer's life better—for example, does it give a better user experience, or does it enable them to get the desired results faster or make those results last longer? If you believe that your brand's advantage does make your consumer's life better, then focus your communication on this. You will certainly piss off the competition, but more importantly, you will do it in a way that builds your brand where it really matters—among your consumers.

Fancy moves never won a street fight—Learn to be ruthlessly competitive if necessary

This is the part where I totally confuse you by asking you to throw away what I have advised earlier! This is because in marketing, as in most aspects of life, one cannot live by rigid rules, just broad principles, which can and must be tweaked to fit the circumstances. I had advocated caution in dealing with competitive communication, but there is one situation where too much caution can kill you—and that is if you find yourself in a real street fight. I would suggest avoiding this, but sometimes you are forced into it. Suppose you are at a pub and a guy starts making rude comments about your date or spouse. What would you do? Perhaps you could ignore him or move away. What if he tries to grab your partner? You could try to reason with him. Now, what if he actually grabs your partner and pushes you away?

See what I mean? Sometimes you are not looking for a fight, but you are faced with a situation where confrontation is inevitable. In a real-life fight of this sort, it is safe to make some assumptions: first, the other person is probably far more experienced at this than you are; second, he probably has far less to lose, or at least thinks so; and third, you can expect him to fight dirty. The same assumptions hold if you are forced into a street fight in the marketplace. What do I mean by a street fight in the context of marketing? Here are some examples:

1. A PR issue blows up in your face when consumers start complaining of adverse effects from using your product, and you find out that one of your competitors may be "encouraging" them.
2. You turn on the TV and see a competitive ad showing your brand and talking about how it is inferior to another brand.
3. Your launch plans for a new product are leaked and a competitor beats you to market with a copycat product with a similar packaging, proposition and pricing.

Do these scenarios sound outlandish? Well, welcome to the world of real-life marketing. These have all actually happened. If you ever find yourself in such a situation, here are a couple of things you could do:

1. Set your lawyers to work immediately to find out the quickest and best legal recourse available. Marketers are usually loath to work with lawyers, as they seem to have no purpose in life other than preventing them from making the best claims they can. But in a situation like this, your lawyer is your best friend. From recommending the best way to defend your claim to forcing offending competitive material off the air, lawyers can give you ideas that you probably would not think of yourself.

2. Your second best friend is your PR manager, or whoever happens to handle public relations. A lot of PR disasters happen because companies ignore what appear to be isolated individual complaints or rumors until it is too late. With seamless global information flow and the Internet, you can no longer count on seemingly isolated cases remaining that way for long. If damage control is what you need, you need to get your side of the story out fast, and that is where your PR contacts come in.

LESSON 42:
Real fights are over faster than you think—Move quickly and win in the consumer's mind

In the movies, fights seem to go on forever, with huge dramatic leaps, lots of fancy footwork, and usually equal trading of blows between the hero and the bad guy, until somehow the good guy prevails. Real life is somewhat different. Real fights rarely involve equally matched fighters, and the one to win is often the one to strike the first decisive blow. It is the same when you are faced with a competitive threat—whether competition is launching into your stronghold, has just pre-empted your launch or aired advertising that denigrates your brand, the one who gets into the consumer's mind first and fastest wins. In a situation like this, I would not waste weeks or even days finessing plans or seeking a lot of new information—I would go with what I know, and try to win faster in the consumer's mind. In such a fight situation, there are three steps I would recommend you look at:

1. Identify the focused message you want consumers to take away. In a situation where the consumer is being bombarded by messages from you and your competitor (and probably a bunch of other players), it is unrealistic to expect them to internalize each one. Sort through them and somehow distill the core message you want them to take away.

Consumers simply have better things to do with their time, so try to condense what you want to communicate into a one-line message. It could be a claim against the competition or a message showing why your offering is better—just keep it short and simple.

2. Figure out the fastest way of getting this out to your consumer. In a situation like this, the normal media choices may or may not make sense. For example, TV takes some time to build up reach and awareness, so if there are localized media choices that may get your message out faster, you could think of supplementing your normal media choices with these other options. Whether it is a local newspaper, outdoor advertising or radio, do not worry as much about efficiency as about what would get your message out faster than your competition.

3. Track whether your plan is working. A plan like the one outlined above can be expensive and generally wreaks havoc on the people involved in terms of driving them crazy with extra work and stress. So do not continue it any longer than you need to. Figure out as fast as you can whether the competitive issue has gone away, and then get back quickly to doing what you would ideally spend your time on anyway—building your brand.

Surround and conquer: Using multiple media to win with the consumer

Everyone thinks life was simpler in the "old days." But I doubt that is really true. Our parents talk about how things were cheaper when they were young, and how they never had as much money. Have they not heard of inflation? Historians talk about how we are entering a "new" phase of "civilizational conflict." Did anyone forget the Crusades? However, when it comes to marketing, I will grudgingly agree that reaching consumers was probably much simpler before than it seems to be now. A few decades ago, all you had to do was develop a good TV spot and put it on air for a few months, and in no time you would reach all the consumers you wanted.

Unfortunately for us marketers, that does not quite hold true any more. In some countries, TV is increasingly not king. People are spending more time online, and even in countries where the Internet still has low penetration, traditional media like TV have become much more segmented, with many channels targeting different niches. The reality that marketers increasingly have to deal with is media fragmentation—reaching the same number of consumers now is much more difficult than it used to be. And it's going to get worse. Wait until the day when all consumers have the choice to skip your ads altogether. So what is a marketer to do? Chase down each and every new media opportunity? Conclude that TV no longer works and stop advertising on it? Not quite. I wish life were so simple. I cannot offer you one easy answer, but the following three lessons may get you started on the right path.

LESSON 43:
Avoid the trap of doing a little bit of everything

One of the downsides of media fragmentation is that a lot of big corporations and marketing whizzes are doing what they do best—swinging from one extreme end of the pendulum to the other, grabbing onto the latest fad; in short, creating a new flavor of the month. I am always a bit skeptical of anyone proclaiming the dawn of a new paradigm. This can be confusing, if not downright dangerous. It is one thing to recognize that the media environment is changing and that we need to adapt to it, but quite another to make a blanket assumption that "the 30-second ad is dead" or that "we need to totally change our marketing mix." These are statements I have heard marketing professionals use in discussing what these changes mean for us. Marketing can usually be broken down to common sense, if we choose to do so. Yes, the media environment is changing, but the fundamentals have not changed. You need to know the media choices available to help you reach your consumer and then decide how you want to allocate your money among them, but this does not mean being taken in by whatever is being peddled as the latest "paradigm."

The first piece of advice I can offer is to avoid the death trap of marketing plans that spread resources too thinly. This is when, caught up in all the jargon of "changing paradigms," you scatter your marketing money across every single media option you can find: a little bit of TV, a little bit of radio, a few outdoor hoardings here and there, and so on. As a result, on paper you certainly have a plan that looks "holistic" and "surrounds the consumer," but given the reality of limited budgets, it usually amounts to throwing money in so many different directions that it has no real consumer impact in any of them. Where you spend your money of course depends on your product or service and the kind of consumer you are targeting, but most likely the really useful media choices available to you can be counted on the fingers of one hand. The important thing is to be able to identify what these media choices are for you, what each of them brings to the party, and how to allocate your spending among them in a way that reflects this. To be able to do that, the next two lessons may come in handy.

LESSON 44:
Don't throw away good money—Understand and use the concept of ROI

Whether you spend a few hundred dollars on your local newspaper or millions on a national campaign, the truth behind every marketing plan is that there is bound to be some wastage if you look hard enough. The old saying is often true in real-world marketing: only 50% of your marketing budget is really working for you, but you can't be sure which 50%. One of the best ways to get more out of your marketing money is to find out how much return you are getting for every dollar you spend on different activities, and then spend more on the higher return items and less on the ones giving lower returns.

That, in the simplest possible terms, sums up the concept of return on investment (ROI). There are many complex and costly models on the market to help you measure the ROI of your marketing activities, some of which can help you generate very useful information. However, many businesses or entrepreneurs will not have access to, or the willingness to spend on, such techniques, so to them I would recommend falling back on a good alternative: common sense.

1. Know where you are really spending your marketing money. Sounds silly, doesn't it? Of course you know where you are spending your money. Or do you? Every time brand managers look at their budgets, they almost always find something that they would rather not be spending on. Everyone creates buffers, and marketing people are no exception. When a new year begins and marketing budgets need to be set, most marketers err on the side of asking for more rather than less. This could be extra money to cover any additional competitive or promotional activities. The problem is that when the year gets underway, marketers often lose track of where the extra money ends up getting spent. Just see where your buffers are, and you could find a pool of money to spend somewhere that actually builds your business.

2. Look at what has worked for your brand and competitors before. What was your spending mix across media when you were growing

the business? Where are your fastest growing competitors spending their money? This usually gives some easy leads on how you could reallocate your money by indicating the media mix and choices that have proven successful in the past or that are currently favored.

3. If there are emerging media that you think hold potential, but you are worried about completely changing your spending plans, consider investing in testing out the media choices—either new media choices, higher media weights or new in-store activities. That way, you do not need expensive and theoretical models to tell you how you should spend your money—you learn from actual in-market experience. If it works, it builds your business as you learn, and if it fails, at least you have not gambled the entire farm.

LESSON 45:
Prioritization—Use the concept of cascading choices

I am not much into theory, but there is an interesting concept that should be an integral part of any marketer's vocabulary: cascading choices. You can learn more about it from a book called *The New Marketing Mission*, but I will give you a taste of what it is all about. When you become comfortable using it, it can be applied not just in marketing, but in dealing with many other aspects of your life as well. So what is this magic concept? It is relatively simple to explain, but much more difficult to put into practice. The concept of cascading choices says that you should rank in descending order of importance the choices you have, and then work your way down the list, moving to the next item only when you are satisfied that you have done all you can with the more important item. In the all too familiar situation of making spending choices with limited and often shrinking marketing budgets, this is a great way to force yourself to prioritize the most important elements of the marketing mix instead of spreading your money thinly all around.

In a marketing context, you would need to start with an understanding of the various media you could use, and some insight into their relative importance for your brand or category. You may or may not have access to tools that can quantify this, but if nothing else, your judgment, past experience and competitive benchmarking can quickly yield this information. Essentially, if you have followed the last lesson, you should be in a position to have a working list. Suppose the list for your brand reads like this:

1. National TV
2. In-store displays
3. Outdoor advertising
4. National radio
5. Print

The next step is to determine what would be optimal spending levels on each of these for your brand. Imagine that if you had no budget constraints, what would you need to spend on each medium to achieve competitive levels of advertising? The level of spending needed can be derived in any number of ways—what is needed to meet your awareness and reach targets, the levels that have been proven to work for you in the past, the levels at which your key competitors are operating, and so on. Once you have this information, it is time to get cracking on cascading choices.

If you were to follow the concept of cascading choices literally, you would take your marketing budget and allocate the optimum amount to the most important item (TV in this case), and then work your way down to the next item. You would repeat this process until you ran out of money or items to spend on. If the world you live in is anything like the one I work in, the former would happen most of the time!

What does cascading choices offer? It forces us to be ruthlessly selective and decisive, and to allocate spending on the media that matter most.

PRICING

It is amazing the volume of marketing literature that focuses on two of the P's of the marketing mix—positioning and promotion. Admittedly, they are at the core of creating and growing brands, but they are only a part of the story. If you believe that they are all there is to success in a career in marketing, you are likely in for a few nasty surprises. I know of many young marketers who jump into their careers assuming that they are in for a lot of ideation, creativity and advertising. Then at some point in their careers they are hit by the hard reality that they are brand managers, not advertising professionals. As such, their reward system is not based on creating great advertising, but rather on growing their brands on a sustainable basis with a cost structure that allows them to keep investing behind the brand and meet the profit targets set by management. In other words, if you want to be a great marketer, you also need to be at least an adequate businessperson. This means gaining some degree of understanding of aspects of managing a brand that go beyond what is typically considered strictly "marketing work." To do so, you will need to gain an understanding of the other P's of marketing, and one of the critical ones you will face is pricing. Don't worry if finance courses seemed to zoom over your head—my intent is not to transform you into a finance guru, but to highlight some areas where you as a marketer can have a critical role in determining pricing moves for your brand.

The price is right: The art of setting pricing

A good place to start is with the basic question of how you should set pricing for a brand, or go about evaluating whether the current pricing is right or not. Pricing on any brand, if done sensibly, is not just a decision driven by costs and profit needs. Instead, it is part of an overall brand strategy and business model. At the center of any pricing decision should be the strategic choices about what kind of consumers the brand is seeking to target and how it wants to position itself. As such, marketers need to be central players in pricing decisions. As for how you as a marketer could influence pricing decisions for your brand, read on for some pointers.

LESSON 46:
If you don't like getting ripped off, why should they? Price based on the consumer, not just your costs

Here is a true story. Years ago, I knew a senior of mine who worked as a marketing manager in a leading firm. I respected him and looked up to him as something of a role model. One day, when I was at his home, we began talking about buying a computer. He was a great help, as he told me about a couple of options that I had not considered, as well as which ones were available at a better bargain. Soon after, when I was buying my first PC and looking forward to nights of blasting aliens, I was thanking him. Later, sitting in a coffee shop and trading stories about each other's jobs, I saw a different side to him. We were talking about some recent price increases on his brands, and he was vigorously arguing that they were the right thing to do even if they left many members of the team feeling uncomfortable about being priced uncompetitively. His reason? He needed to meet a certain profit margin. It was his job, and I figured he did not need my gratuitous advice on how to do it, but I was left wondering how someone so savvy about value as a consumer could suddenly be so different as a marketer.

I do not blame him, as over the years I have come to understand why marketers sometimes behave as if pricing is a figure to plug into a spreadsheet, not real money they expect consumers to shell out for buying their brands. The reason for such behavior is a word starting with a capital "C". No, not Costs, but Capitalism. Every marketer and every business is expected to make money, and usually it feels like whatever they deliver is never enough.

That may be true, and I cannot wish away business realities, but this is where you as a marketer can start earning your salary in any discussion on pricing. Guess who is most impacted by pricing decisions on your brand? Your consumer. And guess the one person who is never involved in making these decisions—that's right, the consumer.

I would argue that it is the marketer's duty to be the voice of the consumer when it comes to pricing decisions. I am not saying that you have to push for low pricing. There are many great brands built on premium pricing, and as a marketer, good profit margins are a great thing, as they enable you to reinvest sufficiently in your brand. What I am advocating is that you be the one who brings the conversation on pricing back to a consumer-centric focus, and not just on making numbers add up in a spreadsheet. What that means is forcing the decision to be rooted in the strategic choices you are making for the brand—the consumers you want to target, the positioning you want for the brand, and the support model you feel is right for your brand. It is not easy to do, but read on and you may find a few tips to initiate such a conversation.

Price based on your total business model—Don't assume finance will somehow figure it out

Now that I have you scratching your head by saying you should "be the voice of the consumer," let me bring this back to mundane reality by sharing how you could make pricing decisions for your brand. To start with, the biggest mistake you can make as a marketer is to assume that pricing is somehow "finance department work." You may have been terrible at finance in school, but taking this attitude is essentially turning your back on what is a critical decision in your total marketing mix. With the firm belief that abdication of responsibility is worse than incompetence, let us dive right in. Here are three questions to ask yourself when laying the groundwork for any pricing decision:

1. How well do you really understand your target consumers and their value orientation? All consumers want good value; however, good value means different things to different people. Are your consumers willing to pay a little bit extra for getting what they want, or do they usually look for a lower-priced deal? What are the competitive brands they use, and how are they priced relative to the rest of the category? Answering these questions should start to give you an understanding of how important pricing is to your target consumers.

2. What are the financial implications of an offering that meets the consumer's needs and delivers your brand's desired positioning? Consider all of the aspects of your proposition that can be adjusted to help find a profitable balance between these two objectives, including the basic product you offer, the packaging shape and design, and the choices on product esthetics like flavors or fragrances. Balancing these objectives is usually an iterative process. Start with what you feel a pure "consumer-driven" pricing strategy would be. Then layer on what you can offer, and see if those choices enable you to meet the desired pricing and still make the kind of money your management expects. If there is a gap, as there usually will be, ask yourself what is really important to your consumer and then ruthlessly choose what you want to offer, driving out unwanted costs but delivering on the parameters critical to winning with your consumer.

3. Are you clear on the support model you want for your brand? This has to be based on an understanding of your category's fundamentals: where and how does your consumer shop, how do competitors

support their brands, what are the best media vehicles to deliver on your positioning, and how much money are you are likely to have at your disposal. Simplistically, brands in most categories exist along a continuum, from those priced at a high premium that use their higher margins to plow back into enhanced support for the brand, to those priced much lower than average that use only sporadic support other than pricing to drive the brand. Neither is necessarily good or bad, but you need to think strategically about where your brand can win uniquely with your consumer, and use that to help drive decisions on pricing. For example, if your model is to price at a premium but reinvest heavily on advertising, and you know your consumer loves your great product and packaging and does not mind paying more, you would do well to resist pressures to cut price if doing so would mean taking away some of these factors that delight your consumer. Likewise, if your consumer has a tight budget and there are a lot of competitive options available at low price points, you may be committing brand suicide by implementing price increases simply to meet internal financial needs without doing anything to enhance the consumer value of your brand.

LESSON 48:
Get to the point, please—Understand the importance of price points

As a kid, I used to think manufacturers were crazy because of the seemingly insane pricing they had on their products. Why on earth would someone price a product at $9.99 when $10 seemed a nicer, rounder number? Years of capitalist corruption later, I now know why they do it—it is all about the magic of price points. In setting the price for your offering, and indeed contemplating any potential pricing move, understanding price points is something that becomes essential. There are really two ways of looking at price points: perceived price points in the consumer's mind, and real price points dictated by coinage. As a marketer, you need to be aware of both to make well-informed pricing decisions.

Psychological price points are sometimes intuitive, like $10 versus $9.99, but sometimes you need to dig a bit deeper to understand what the price points in your category may be. They may be defined by simplistic "round numbers," but also by the consumer's competitive benchmarks. The best way of understanding price points is to get a full picture of the pricing landscape that your consumer faces—determine what competitive offerings are available to them at different price points, and then overlay what seem to be intuitive or coinage-linked price points. If the market-leading brand is available at a price of $20, consumers are probably more likely to consider trying another brand that is at or below this price point than they are to consider brands priced at higher round numbers like $30 or $40.

The second category of price points is related to the coinage used in the market. This is especially important in some developing markets where products are often sold in low cash outlay units. For example, in Vietnam, where the currency is the dong, a whole host of trial-sized packs and single-use units are available at price points like 500 and 1,000 dong. The shocking realization is that there is no coinage in between these two amounts. That throws traditional thinking on pricing, which often operates on raising prices to cover inflation or costs, out the window. If you are playing in this segment at 500 dong, the only increase you can take is to double your price at one stroke! Knowledge of the local market, and an understanding of the trends of which price points are coming in or being phased out, can help you stay ahead of the game.

You're going down! The tricky business of pricing down

Anyone who understands the rudiments of demand and supply will assume that when you take prices down, volume will go up. However, the harsh reality is that most pricing moves do not work and are fraught with danger.

The financial implications aside, one of the reasons price decreases do not work is that the reduction is often not meaningful from a consumer standpoint. You may have satisfied yourself by taking prices down, but you have not made any real change in price point for the consumer. Even if you have found a good lower price point to decrease to, only half the battle is won. There are some real barriers to making pricing work.

LESSON 49:
Pay it forward—Make sure that price changes pass through to your consumer

One of the most common reasons that pricing moves do not work is that the consumers often do not get to see it. There are usually two important reasons for this. The first is the basic issue of awareness. You may have decided to take prices down, but do your consumers know that? As a rule of thumb, a price down that is not advertised is unlikely to work, simply because most price downs depend on attracting new users to the brand, and without awareness of the new pricing, that is unlikely to happen. A good exercise is to think of a price down just as you would think of introducing a new item or launching a new campaign. Doing so will force you to think of the basics, such as how much awareness you would need, what media vehicles you would want, which consumers you are trying to attract and so on. In addition, do not assume that what you want to communicate is a no-brainer. Price communication is as legitimate a marketing task as advertising any other benefit or attribute and needs to be approached with the same discipline. Suppose you are reducing your price from $12 to $9.99. What is the one thing you would want consumers to take away: a 17% price reduction, or the new price point of $9.99? In practice, if the price point you are moving to is considered a "magic" price point (such as the one in this example), you are better off focusing on the price point itself instead of the discount. On the other hand, if your new price point has no real "magic" associated with coinage or a competitive benchmark, driving home the reduction may well work better.

Even if you have plans in place to generate awareness among your desired consumers, you will need to tackle the second barrier that usually comes in the way of a successful price reduction: the problem of the man in the middle. Whether you are dealing with packaged goods on a supermarket shelf or services, the reality is that most of your offerings reach end consumers through intermediaries, whether they are agents, distributors or retailers. When you reduce your prices, these intermediaries typically make less money on each transaction than they would have before. Put yourself in their shoes and think of why you would want to pass on the lower pricing to the consumer, especially since in most markets, legal regulations allow marketers to enforce only a "suggested" retail price. The lesson here is that when you plan a price down, you need a story for the intermediary that lays out how they will benefit from passing the lower price through to end consumers. The benefit could be more money in absolute terms as more consumers come into the brand, or it could be incentives linked to passing through the new pricing. Making a price down work is not easy, and it is no surprise that so many of them do not succeed.

LESSON 50:
Sounds too good to be true? Balance price and equity communication

If you are trying to understand how people perceive the trade-off between price and perceived quality, a great place to start is to browse through online auctions. Over the last couple of months I had been doing quite a bit of that, trying to both buy and sell, as part of an attempt to refurbish my place. I remember a lot of listings where the price seemed way too low, and the glowing descriptors of "in brand new shape, rarely used" did little to dispel the nagging feeling that I was being offered a lemon. That is one of the biggest risks you face as a marketer when you communicate that your brand is available at a lower price. Simply put, the risk is that the consumer asks one of two questions:

1. What have you taken out, or what am I losing out on?
2. If the product or service is the same as before, why were you taking me for a ride all this time by charging a higher price?

Effectively balancing this trade-off between price and perceived quality involves understanding that consumer value is not just the price at which your brand is available, but also something broader and intangible. It is a combination of pricing and the perceived benefits that your brand offers. So if you are taking a price down, remember that your ultimate task is not just to decrease the price, but also to improve consumer value. By definition, that means that you need to balance communicating the lower price with what your brand offers. Ideally, the communication should be a good balance of the benefit or offering that differentiates your brand, and the pricing. That balance depends in part on the market realities facing your brand and the reasons you are considering a price down in the first place.

If yours is an established brand that already stands for something in the consumer's mind, and pricing down is an attempt to make its otherwise desirable benefits more accessible to consumers, then you may not need to go overboard in communicating what the brand offers. A message along the lines of "the benefits you always wanted are now available at great value" may work just fine. On the other hand, if yours is a smaller brand, with less clearly established equities, then screaming pricing alone may just generate the kind of reactions I had when I saw some of the online auction listings. In such a case, it is important to be more deliberate in communicating what the brand stands for in addition to giving information about the new pricing. Sounds challenging? You bet it is. Which is why ideally you should wait until your brand stands for something before trying to play pricing games, otherwise no matter what you say in you advertising, the consumer may hear just one word—lemon.

But they started it! The even trickier business of dealing with price competitors

It seems to be a fact of life that in every group, there is always someone who loves stirring things up. In school, I remember a kid who for no conceivable reason would pick fights with other boys, trouble the girls, bother the teachers, and in general wreak havoc all around. In the world of grown-ups, things seem to be little different. For every quiet soccer fan, there seems to be a loutish zealot, and for every responsible drinker at a bar, there seems to be one who has had way too many. I have no idea why this is so, other than supposing that it does take all sorts to make the world the way it is. The marketplace also holds such a special class of troublemakers for marketers—price competitors. Usually brands with lower advertising and marketing budgets, little original innovation other than trying to keep up with existing trends, and leaner cost structures than larger competitors, they use pricing as their primary weapon. Marketers sometimes dismiss them as troublemakers out to make the category a commodity, but I feel they serve an important role. They challenge our thinking as marketers, forcing us to ask what wasted costs we have that compel us to charge a much higher price, and also making us prove our worth as marketers by convincing consumers to prefer something that costs more money.

LESSON 51:
Understand, don't dismiss price competitors

The basic human instinct when faced with something unfamiliar is to try to reframe it in familiar terms. Marketers are no different. The biggest mistake most mainstream marketers make while looking at price competitors is to assume that they are somehow inferior. When faced with a much lower-priced competitor, the usual temptation is to either dismiss it ("the product must be crap") or to think that it is impossible to match the costs. Both are dangerous conclusions. The first may lead marketers to underestimate a serious threat, while the second may be turning a blind eye to inefficiency in their own systems. Buy not every price competitor needs to be taken with the same degree of seriousness—after all, there are often genuinely crappy offerings that enter a market hoping to sell on little other than cut-throat pricing and exit just as quietly. But at the same time, every category has some brands that turn the value equation in the category upside down to their favor.

During a war, the best commanders are the ones who try to get into the minds of their adversaries and think like them. In understanding price competitors, you need a similar approach. The first step is to put yourself in their shoes and construct what you think their structure looks like. What do you think their product costs? How much do they spend on marketing? What is their pricing? With a few such simple questions based largely on publicly available information like media spending, raw material costs, etc, you could create a picture of what their cost structure looks like with a fair bit of accuracy.

The next step is benchmarking. Put your offerings side by side and see where your costs lie in comparison. The point is not to emulate, but to understand two things. First, is there any waste in your system that you could strip out to offer better value to your consumer? Does your product or packaging have frills that you could afford to lose, or is your marketing budget way too flabby? The second important purpose of this exercise is to identify what choices they may be making that are different from yours? Are they just accepting lower profit margins? Are they spending their money on activities very different from yours? Understanding this will give a clearer picture of what your unique strengths and weaknesses are versus a price competitor.

LESSON 52:
Play to your strengths and business model, not to every competitive move

When facing a price competitor, whatever you do, do not abandon your strengths and end up playing by your competition's rules. When you have done your benchmarking, you should understand your price competitor better. However, this does not mean that you should blindly assume that the path to assured success lies in somehow matching the pricing. Usually, the smarter play is to understand what your competitive advantage is— simply put, what can you do better than your competition, or what can you do that your competitor will not be able to copy easily? Against a price competitor, your competitive advantage may be the ability to offer a truly superior product, the ability to advertise much more heavily, or the ability to generate a stronger pipeline of new ideas and innovation. Whatever it is, know it and play it for all it is worth.

Sometimes you may be up against a really tough price competitor who has more than just low pricing on its side. Perhaps it is able to bring better local consumer and customer understanding to the table, or perhaps it has great depth of distribution that you cannot easily match. Whatever the reason, there will be times when you may find that playing by your usual rules is not enough. In such a situation, the answer is not to change your entire business model overnight, as there is a way you could still play to win this game.

LESSON 53:
Using specialized offerings to fight price competitors

Instead of trying to change everything about your brand and business model, it is sometimes possible to use specialized offerings to take on price competitors. This may be in the form of a lower-priced sub-line on your brand or a new brand altogether. In either case, the basic principle is the same—create a specialized offering that plays by the rules of the price competitor without risking your base business. In designing a totally new offering to do so, you could learn a lot from the benchmarking exercise mentioned earlier, using this information to identify product and marketing choices that you could make to achieve the same kind of pricing as your competitor. However, your real source of competitive advantage comes not just from launching a lower-priced offering, but from the skills and capabilities you can borrow from your base brand.

Creating a lower-priced offering to compete with a price competitor is a good first step, but then equipping it with some of your base brand's superior capabilities may be the decisive advantage you need. These capabilities may include the ability to advertise at higher levels by borrowing from your more profitable base brand, access to better consumer understanding and research, and a stronger pipeline of new ideas—all advantages that larger, more profitable brands typically have compared to price competitors.

There's no such thing as a free lunch: Pricing up

A re you familiar with the Greek myth of Icarus? He was a rather dedicated young lad, who resolved to help his father, Daedalus, escape imprisonment by constructing wings of feather and wax. With this homemade flying apparatus, they set out on their flight to safety. His father warned him not to fly too high, but once they took flight, Icarus was so spellbound by the experience that he kept trying to go higher. He started his journey with the best of intentions, but he did not heed the warning signs that he was getting too close to the sun. What happened next was inevitable, as what goes up must come down, which in this case was a burning mass of charred feathers and molten wax. What does this have to do with marketing? Simply that when marketers think of pricing up, they need to think of themselves as Icarus. Their objectives may be noble, like improving profitability, being able to give their consumers a better product or experience, or being able to spend more on media, but when they get carried away in pricing up, like Icarus, they get burned.

Price based on consumer price points, not spreadsheet indices

I would not be too hard on Icarus—he was having a blast, and flying even higher among the clouds must have seemed an irresistible temptation to the young man. Now just imagine if he had an altimeter and a clear guideline that if he went above a certain height, he would be in danger. I am sure there would have been a very different end to this myth, since I am assuming he was not flying toward the sun as part of an elaborate suicide plot. As a marketer, there will be times when you have to take prices up. If nothing else, exchange rates, escalating costs and inflation alone will dictate this. The thing to take away from this lesson is not whether you should price up or not, but rather that when you do price up, you should do so with an altimeter strapped firmly to your wrist. In this case, the altimeter is the knowledge of price points.

So next time you hear someone say something like, "We need to take a 5% price increase," steer the conversation away from percentages plucked from spreadsheets and toward what that decision means in terms of consumer price points. When faced with a decision to price up, here are a couple of suggestions:

1. The first thing you could try to do is to meet your financial objectives while not crossing any consumer-meaningful price points. In doing so, you could apply a lot of the things we talked about in Lesson 47. First, fix the price point you want to meet, and then challenge yourself and your team on what unwanted costs you could drive out to meet your financial objectives while not crossing this price point. Often, you will find waste in the system, either in the form of product features that the consumer does not really want or in wasted marketing costs.

2. So what do you do when you are faced with the reality of crossing a consumer-relevant price point? One thought is to apply all of the principles we talked about in Lesson 20 regarding making relaunches work. You can then see what you can offer that makes a positive impact on how the consumer experiences your brand, such as bundling the price increase with an improvement in your packaging, a new proposition, better service, etc.

Sweetening the mix—Make premium-priced items your best friend

One of the tough realities facing most marketers is the seeming inevitability of having to take prices up contrasted with the ever-present consumer desire for better value. Sometimes it is possible to make the higher pricing a virtue by improving the consumer proposition or experience, so that total consumer value ends up being better, not worse. Sadly, this is not always possible. In a situation like this, or when you feel that taking prices up on your total brand beyond a point would be suicidal, you need to make friends with premium-priced items.

An example is business and first class in airlines. If airlines were to offer all of their seats at the high prices of business or first class, they would likely find few takers. But by balancing the higher volumes from economy class with the higher value per unit of business and first class, they are able to achieve higher overall profitability than they would by offering all economy class.

As a marketer, you can play an important role in identifying such opportunities for your business. The basic question you need to ask is whether there is a segment of your target consumers that would be willing to pay more money for an enhanced offering. These could be consumers who have a higher need for the benefit your brand offers (e.g. consumers with more damaged hair or skin), are more intense users of the category (e.g. frequent business travelers), or simply have much higher disposable incomes than the bulk of your consumers. Once you have this group in mind, it is not enough to just offer the same product or service at a higher price and then assume they will readily pay more. Chances are these will be more discerning than the average consumer, and you need to lead the thinking on which attributes or features they will be looking for that set them apart from the average consumer. Using these two pieces of knowledge can yield a powerful benefit for your brand—the ability to tap into a more profitable segment, while not risking the bulk of your current business with higher pricing. An added advantage of this is that advertising these premium items tends to have a halo effect on the entire business. Have you ever wondered why airlines often focus their advertising on features like flat beds that are only found in business or first class? Advertising the attributes of the premium offering reflects well on the overall brand, thereby allowing you to increase your brand's overall equity as well as your profits.

LESSON 56:
Money can't buy you love—Use reframing to make money no object

A common mistake is to equate value with pricing. As a result, when marketers talk of improving value, the first instinct seems to be to reduce pricing. Nothing could be farther from the truth. One of the oldest axioms in marketing is that you do not really sell a product or service, but rather what you sell most often is hope. Hope for a slimmer figure, hope for fairer skin, hope for more prestige, hope for more sex appeal. Hope sells, and nothing makes pricing more irrelevant than tapping into some of our deepest hopes. Look at premium brands like Mercedes, Mont Blanc or Chanel and you will realize that value means much more than low pricing. That is because their consumers are buying into something much more than just the physical product. They are differentiated from cheaper offerings in their category, not just by the physical differences in their products, but also on intangible yet very real differences in the emotional payoff that they offer their users.

This need not be restricted to super premium brands. Each and every brand can use these same principles to drive value for their consumers beyond pricing. All you need to do is to ask yourself some simple questions:

1. What emotional needs are your consumers seeking to fulfill by using your brand? An understanding of this can unleash a very powerful form of reframing, allowing you to link your brand to some deeper payoff that makes the money you charge seem trivial. Are you selling car tires, or are you selling safety for the driver's family? Are you really selling a skin care product, or are you selling the approval of one's partner? Are you selling sanitary napkins, or greater self-confidence?
2. What are the gold standards of performance in your category and can you reframe in relation to them? If you can find a product or process that consumers regard as being the best for delivering your category benefits, but which is too expensive for regular use, you may be sitting on a goldmine. All you need to do is make the connection that your brand makes these benefits more accessible—like a shampoo offering salon-quality hair at home.

3. What could your consumers be missing out on if they don't get the benefits of your brand? The fear of negative consequences is a very powerful motivator, and is an integral part of every marketer's arsenal. Not for nothing did mouthwashes and deodorants take off when they started talking about the negative social consequences of bad odor.

PRODUCT

The scientist is not a person who gives the right
answers; he is the one who asks the right questions.
— Claude Levi-Strauss

If pricing seems to be an odd topic for a book on brand management, then product must seem an even stranger subject. But only if you have a very narrow view of a product being something cooked up by scientists in labs and handed over to marketers to bring to market. As a marketer in the real world, you have a critical role to play in influencing this "P" of your marketing mix. It begins with how you can, and should, influence the process of developing new products by ensuring that it is rooted in what your consumers value and not just driven by technology developments. A marketer also plays a huge role in determining the pace and nature of innovation needed to win in the marketplace. Product innovation is not just the ability to bring new ideas to the market, but also the ability to know how often this should happen—something that you as a marketer are best equipped to answer. The marketer's role may not be in developing the product *per se*, but in bringing the right questions to the table. This chapter covers these aspects, as well as situations in which too much product innovation may be a bad thing and how you as a marketer could deal with that.

But I flunked science! A marketer's role in product design

When I was studying in school in India, the default option after Grade 10 if you had reasonable grades was to study science, which acted as a stepping-stone to studying engineering or medicine. Those who studied commerce were considered an acceptable second class, but those who studied humanities were decidedly at the bottom of this informal caste system, with the implicit assumption that you were doing so because you did not have the smarts to compete in science. I passed Grade 10 with decent results, and like most kids of that age, I had no idea what I wanted to do with my life. What I did know was what I did not want to be: one of the nerdy, studious kids who seemed to have little in their lives beyond slaving away at engineering entrance exams and spending time in sterile labs. I had always liked history and literature, and so I chose to study humanities, much to the horror of most of my teachers and classmates. As a result, while I enjoy reading about topics like astronomy, I have little by way of a formal education in the sciences. While other marketers may have studied science in school or even college, the fact is that by training or profession, they are not experts in what goes into the making of the product or service they offer. What then could they bring to a discussion involving product? Lots, simply because this is no longer the exclusive province of scientists in a lab, but has become an integral part of the marketing mix, where marketers can, and must, play a pivotal role.

LESSON 51:
Make sure that product attributes mirror your desired equities

The Internet is a wonderful thing, and has opened up opportunities for learning and networking that earlier generations could only have dreamed of. However, one aspect of the Internet that is much overstated is its utility in finding love. Yes, there are hundreds of chat rooms and dating sites where people surf looking for company or true love. However, the Internet has historically been a bad place for finding lasting love. The biggest reason for this is that most people log in to websites and chat rooms with profiles they feel would make them attractive to others, but which may have little resemblance to their real selves. So a 45-year-old father of two, with a balding pate and a beer belly advertises himself as a 28-year-old who works out every day, and a 53-year-old spinster transforms into a 22-year-old college girl who likes partying. This works for meeting new people and chatting, but if you are looking for true love, it is a bit like a box of chocolates—you never know quite what you'll get. In marketing terms, this is a case of a mismatch between what is promised or advertised and what the product or service can deliver.

This is one key area where you as a marketer can influence product design in an important way. When you have applied the lessons on positioning, you should be able to come up with the single-minded proposition that you want to leave your consumers with. As a marketer, your role does not end there. You may get consumers to try your brand, but if what they experience upon doing so does not meet their expectations, they will move on just as quickly. Making sure that your product or service experience matches what you want your consumers to associate with your brand is not difficult by itself. What is difficult is changing the mindset from thinking that marketing is just about demand generation, to recognizing that marketing is about getting consumers into your brand and then retaining them. Ensuring a fit between pre- and post-usage expectations is a key requirement for customer retention. In planning how to ensure this alignment of expectations, take the following into consideration:

1. Be clear on the one or two attributes that you want to differentiate your brand from the competition, and communicate this information clearly to those designing the product or service.
2. When testing the product or service, make sure you are not just looking to see whether consumers like the offering, but also that the reason they like it is in line with the attributes you want your brand associated with.
3. Benchmark your product or service against the competition to ensure that your brand's experience is not being designed in a competitive vacuum.

LESSON 58:
Watch for over-engineered products not based on consumer needs

When it comes to marketing, more is not necessarily better. We saw how being single-minded is critical to developing a winning proposition, and that same need to make clear choices holds true for product design as well. That is where a marketer can play another critical role in product design—in addition to ensuring that the product includes everything the consumer is looking for, a marketer should also be asking whether there are frills that the consumer does not really care about. You may wonder why this is important, since extra features must surely be a good thing. The reason is that there is indeed no such thing as a free lunch, and if your offering comes packed with features that are not important to your consumer, there is a huge opportunity loss. You could take that cost and either make your product available at better value or reinvest it on features that count, or just choose to make more money.

This highlights the change in mindset I talked about earlier—as a brand manager or marketer, you are not there just to make advertising or execute marketing plans. You need to think of yourself as a true custodian of the brand, ensuring that every aspect of your brand is truly in line with what your consumer wants. Part of this is plain common sense and survival instinct: if your offering has a lot of unwanted frills, sooner or later this will show in the brand's results, either when a cheaper competitor cleans your house or when competition outspends you because they have not invested in unnecessary product features.

In an environment of increasing costs, this can really set you, and your brand, apart. In the future, the marketer who challenges costs and tries to drive waste out of the system will have a distinct edge over others. The short-term advantage of cutting unnecessary features is that it allows you to give better value to your consumer, or spend more on growing your brand. On a personal level, the longer-term payoff for you is that when your management looks at whether you have the potential to rise to the top, this ability to see the bigger picture beyond just marketing really counts.

LESSON 59:
Barking up the wrong tree—Understand real consumer usage habits and considerations

Aside from understanding how your product measures against direct competitors, another key factor in product design is knowing how you stack up against "indirect" competitors. This is where consumer understanding and insights can play a critical role.

Suppose you are trying to sell breakfast cereal, and have been called in by the R&D people to help identify what they should benchmark your product against. The obvious solution would be to benchmark tastes, flavors and whatever else is important to cereal consumers to competitive cereals on the market. The less obvious solution is that your cereal may not just be competing against other cereals, but against all of the options that consumers have for breakfast. Many multinationals learned this the hard way in several Asian markets, where they found it tough to shift consumers from traditional foods to the relatively new and alien concept of breakfast cereals.

This is something that holds true across categories. Sometimes consumers see soft drinks, coffee and beer as alternatives; see budget airlines as an alternative to trains; and video games as an alternative to movies. The common thread is that consumers do not always limit their purchase decisions to individual categories, but rather make purchases to satisfy needs, even if this means looking to an unexpected category. The problem is that manufacturers tend to think largely on the basis of their specific categories and product segments.

This is where you bring marketing expertise into the discussion and focus on what need you are trying to satisfy, as this will help identify where the real competition is. Once this is clear, it becomes easier to design your offering and proposition to better meet this need than the competition.

Cooking 101: Making a product launch a reality

I am quite a foodie. I love eating good food and I love cooking. This weakness leaves me literally on a treadmill, fighting a seemingly endless battle against being overweight. One of the things I like about cooking is that it gives me huge satisfaction to transform seemingly bland ingredients into something mouth-watering, and then the pleasure of serving others something that delights them. When you think of it that way, cooking is not all that different from marketing, is it? Pushing this analogy further, developing and launching a new product or offering is the closest you get to cooking in the marketing context, as you go through all of the same stages— figuring out what to cook, gathering the raw materials, mixing them together in a way that will satisfy your customer, and finally serving it in a way that does justice to all the effort you have put into cooking it. So for the rest of this chapter, imagine that you and I have started a restaurant together. We have a great location and the necessary financing, so now we are getting into the meat of the issue—the food we serve.

Too many cooks aren't always bad—Recognize that marketing alone won't get the job done

In deciding the menu for our restaurant, one of the basic facts we will have to deal with is that there is no chef in the world who is a master of every type of food. Hence, to make our restaurant succeed, we will have to figure out the types of cuisine we want to serve and then look for chefs with expertise in different areas. For example, if we decide we are going to serve Indian food, I would love to get a chef who is known for his expertise in main courses like tandoori and kebabs, and someone else who has expertise in desserts. Most Indian restaurants I have been to around the world seem to totally neglect the vast array of traditional Indian desserts, and settle for the lowest common denominator simply because they have a chef who may do a pretty good job of the main courses, but just knows a few standard desserts. For anyone out there who is contemplating opening an Indian restaurant, a free idea is to serve the full array of authentic desserts from around India. But I digress; so let me get back to my analogy.

In launching or developing a new product, it is tempting to assume that once the scientists or designers have figured it out, hopefully with a lot of input from you, all that remains to be done is to develop a great marketing plan and you will have a surefire success on your hands. Unfortunately, the real world is a bit more complicated than that. Someone actually has to produce whatever it is that you want to sell, someone may have to register it with government or regulatory bodies before you can make a single sale, and someone needs to make sure that whatever you want to name your offering is trademark-protected so that another company cannot rip off your idea the next day. There are many other things that need to be done to make any launch a reality, but you get the picture. Marketing is usually just one cog in the wheel, albeit an important one, for getting any launch off the ground. The challenge for marketers is to avoid a narrow, marketing-centric view of what a launch entails, and to recognize that they must work hand-in-hand with their colleagues in other departments and leverage their expertise to make the launch a success.

Plan for a buffet, serve *à la carte*—Start with a broad set of ideas, and then narrow them down

Choosing what items to have on our menu will be the next question we tackle. It can be a tough decision: offering too many items may be more than you can handle, while offering too few may mean that you miss out on some items that could have been bestsellers. I have no experience in running a restaurant, but here is an idea that may get us started. Let's serve only a buffet for the first couple of weeks, and keep serving different dishes every couple of days. After a few days, we will get a feel for which are the most popular dishes and make them a regular feature of our *à la carte* menu. Sounds like a plan? I do not know whether we could actually make this work in a real restaurant, but as a marketer you may use a similar approach when deciding which offerings you take to market.

A common problem in deciding on what products or offerings to launch is that there are often many available options. Some may have emerged from new technologies or processes, others may have resulted from brainstorming among the marketing team, and some ideas may have been sparked by looking at what competitors are doing. Regardless of where the ideas come from, one of the core decisions is to choose which will make it to market, and which will not. The answer is actually quite simple: just follow the same approach as our restaurant. Start off with as many ideas as you can—the more the merrier. Do not use any screening at this stage. Just have everyone in your team throw all of their pet ideas on the table, and also look at what other brands are doing to determine whether there is anything you can reapply from them. Then serve these ideas up in a big buffet—in other words, get them in front of your consumers. Use feedback from focus groups, quantitative research or placing prototypes with prospective consumers to screen these ideas and reduce them to a smaller number. Then look at which ones best meet your business and financial needs and which can be brought to market given your current technical capability, and then decide the order in which you launch them. This way, you ensure that you always have a few ideas up your sleeve in case some get delayed or do not work out. Furthermore, starting the process with a broad focus will force you and your team to look beyond just the obvious ideas.

LESSON 62:

A bad waiter can undo the best dish—Understand and help bust bottlenecks that may get in the way, even if they aren't marketing related

I am sure you must have had an experience where you decided never to go to a restaurant again because of a rude waiter, even though the food may have been great. That is something we need to keep in mind as we plan our restaurant. While cooking great food is at the core of making it successful, it is by no means the only factor we need to look at. What ultimately matters is the total experience our consumers have when they step into our restaurant and order our food. The quality of the food matters a lot, but then so do things like the ambience, the service time, the way the food is presented, the attitude of the waiters, and so on. If we really want this restaurant to succeed, we need to pay as much attention to these aspects as we do to the food. It is no different in marketing. A whole host of factors that are ordinarily outside of "marketing" can make or break your launch, such as how the product looks in-store, the rate at which stocks are replenished, and, in many service related industries, the human face of your brand when consumers actually experience it.

This is one critical lesson you should not forget, since most textbooks will not teach you much about it. Marketing is NOT just about brilliant strategies and positioning choices—it is equally about the quality of execution. In the real-world marketplace, the success of any new launch can be undermined by shoddy execution, no matter how breakthrough the thinking and strategies behind it may have been. Marketers need to think of their role as slightly broader than just cooking up the marketing strategies and plans. In making any new product launch a success, one of the roles a marketer has to play is to make sure that all of the other cogs of the wheel are working in sync to deliver the desired results. I am not suggesting that marketers need to do all of this work themselves; however, you need to take a broader view of the marketing mix that incorporates all of these elements related to execution, and ensure that whoever needs to deliver on these steps actually does so. Does this mean marketers end up spending some of their time chasing other departments and coordinating their work? Yes. As a brand manager, you are the custodian of your brand—the general manager of your own little business empire—and anything that comes in the way of success should be something that bothers you. This is the attitude that distinguishes a great marketer and a great new product launch from those that fall short.

Another "P" of marketing: Pace—setting the right rhythm of "news"

The title of this chapter is borrowed from a business magazine article I read many years ago. In typical breathless "here's the latest fad" tone, the article proclaimed there was a new "P" that all marketers need to take on board—something called "pace." The article was essentially advocating that marketers need to step up the pace of innovation or "news" on their brands, and make sure that they are not being out-innovated by competition. This can be a dangerous piece of advice if not taken with enough salt. The problem is that in the real world, to many marketers pace means only one thing—increasing the pace of product launches. Don't get me wrong, innovation is great and every category thrives on it to some extent, but there is such a thing as running too fast. The answer is not to blindly throw new ideas or items into the marketplace, but rather to recognize the right pace that your category and consumer need.

LESSON 63:

The disease called "Launch-itis"—Continually launching new items is not always smart

Every year, thousands of new items flood markets around the world—some are brands that are completely new to the world, but the majority are simply new flavors, extensions or variants of existing brands. The reason for this is not so difficult to understand when you realize that marketers are doing their jobs in return for rewards, and the reward system in most organizations, especially at the junior levels, is essentially based on short-term activity and results. So there is a natural tendency to show that one is "doing something," and in the marketing context, unfortunately that often means launching "new" items. Launching new items is not a bad thing, and it can be an important way of growing your business. However, before you jump on the "get something new into the market" bandwagon, you may want to consider the following.

1. Is launching the new item going to help you get new users into your brand or get existing users to use more of your brand in a way that your current offering would not? An example could be introducing a diet version of a cola to target health-conscious drinkers who may otherwise shy away from the calorie-laden mother brand.

2. Is your base business declining, growing or stable? The worst reason to launch a new item is to correct a decline in your base business, since the launch will likely not help address the fundamental equity or other issues behind it, and may even distract from fixing the existing problems. When your house is on fire, you focus on putting it out, not on thinking of building a bigger garage.

3. Does your new item allow you to make claims that you cannot make on your base brand? Sometimes, you may have better technology or claims that would be too expensive or complex to use on the total brand, but launching them on a new item may allow claims that have a halo effect on the total brand. An example we discussed earlier is the way an airline often advertises features available on first class to create a halo effect on the airline as a whole.

Setting the speed limit—Understand the pace requirements of your market

I don't have anything against innovation. I'm just against frenzied and reckless launches of new items. The "pace" at which you bring new products into the market should not be determined by the latest management fads, business magazine articles, or whims of a brand manager with too much spare time. It should be based on something integral to your brand's success—the needs of your consumers. Consider the following to determine the right pace for your consumers.

1. Understand the rate of change of consumer habits and needs in your category. To take an extreme example, contrast personal computing with condoms. In the former, the needs of users have been rapidly changing and evolving every couple of years, in many instances leading to new innovation to address these needs—a good example being wireless solutions for greater portability. The latter serves a need that has not changed much since Adam met Eve, and while there have certainly been innovations, the extent to which evolving needs have driven these is obviously much lower than for personal computing.

2. Know the likelihood of rapid technological change in your category. Consumer needs drive innovation, but sometimes the availability of new, revolutionary technologies can spur on a new stream of innovation. Understanding what your scientists have in the works and what your competitors are developing could give you clues as to whether a major disruption is around the corner in your category.

3. Understand the role your consumers' shopping and usage habits play in driving the need for news. How often are your consumers in the market choosing between alternative offerings? As a rule of thumb, the more often consumers have the chance to change their brand preference, the greater the need for news. What are loyalty levels like in your category? In some categories, consumers tend to stay with a purchase for much longer given the investment or stakes involved; in others, consumers may change much more often due to lower switching costs and a lower risk to trying something new. For example, packaged consumer goods typically need faster churn of news compared to categories that lock in consumers for much longer periods, like investment products at banks.

There are always exceptions to any rule, but if you heed the above suggestions for your brand and category you will be more comfortable addressing the question of finding the right pace for your brand.

LESSON 65:
Learn to build on big ideas instead of jumping to the next big thing

Once you have identified a big idea and brought it to market, the usual tendency is to start looking for the next big thing. This is not unique to marketing, but is found in most fields of human endeavor. Whether it is continually looking for a better job, a better house, or a better partner, the search seems endless. In a way, being dissatisfied with what we have is good, as that is one of the drivers of innovation and progress. However, looking for better ways of doing something should not mean we abandon everything that has come before it. It is very much the same in marketing; if you have had the good fortune, or perhaps the great marketing acumen, to come up with a big idea that really gets consumers flocking to your brand, do yourself and your brand a big favor and pause before you start looking for the next item to launch.

The risk of not doing so is that you could, without realizing it, accumulate a whole gaggle of items in your brand's line-up that you do not continue to support on any sustained basis. In the crowded consumer product marketplace with limited shelf space and an ever- increasing population of new items, this will mean that at some point retailers will start asking you to remove slow-moving items to avoid wasting in-store shelf space with items that do not sell.

Even if you conclude that your consumer needs a frequent dose of news, do not assume this has to mean identifying and launching a whole host of new items. The trick is not to swing to an extreme. By all means, launch new items if you have a consumer need you can tap into, or you get a new technology to commercialize. But at the same time, keep asking yourself what you could do to drive your business using existing ideas. There are two simple questions to keep asking yourself:

1. Is there a way that I could get new users to use this existing offering? Lessons 11 and 12 could be a good place to start thinking about how to make this happen.
2. Can I get existing users to use more of this offering? Lesson 10 would be a good place to start in addressing this question.

Just as important as understanding how to create a successful product launch is learning to harness the power of commercializing existing items and products so that they deliver as much growth, and sometimes even higher growth, than launching new items. The next chapter will give you some tips on how to go about this.

Perception is reality: The power of marketing vs. product innovation

The last chapter cautioned against relying on launching new items alone as a means to keep your brand growing. Now, imagine what would happen if you were not able to launch a new item? What would you do? Sometimes the best way to think of solutions is to create a scenario where you do not really have an alternative. This "scarcity mentality" works wonders because it forces you to think of choices you may otherwise never consider. In many ways, the ability to grow a brand without relying on new technology or new product launches is the acid test of a marketer. Given that new launches are increasingly costly and technological breakthroughs are all too infrequent and hard to come by, growing a brand without these things is a skill that could really set you and your brand apart.

LESSON 66:
Hidden talents—Rediscover your product before looking for a new one

Sometimes you think you know someone so well that it seems there is nothing you do not know about the person. But then something happens that allows you to see that person in a totally new light. I think it is the same with all of us—there are some sides of our personality that we just do not expose to others, sometimes out of choice, and sometimes because these aspects come out only in exceptional circumstances. I thought I knew my grandfather quite well, and on his 80th birthday, the entire extended family gathered to celebrate. I knew the old man was a stickler for rules and discipline, so when I asked him what he wanted to do on his birthday, I was shocked when he pulled me aside and said he had not had a good drink in decades, and would love to have a beer and some fried fish with me. That evening as we sat on the roof, away from some disapproving relatives, and drank and chatted about stories from his youth, I learned of a whole new dimension to my grandfather's personality, and I still cherish the fact that he chose to share it with me. The secret to unleashing the power of marketing innovation is to uncover and use such hidden insights about your current product or offering instead of waiting for the next new product.

You may think that your current product is "old," but when you take a closer look you are bound to uncover different features, aspects or dimensions to its performance that you may not have noticed before. Then see how you can marry these with unmet consumer needs; do this, and you have the recipe for great marketing innovation. The key is to start with the end in mind—ask yourself what consumer needs, trends or competitive opportunities you are seeking to tap into. Once you are clear on that, lock yourself in a room with your R&D people and anyone else on your team who knows the brand and ask the following question: If all you had was your current product or technology, how could you use it to tap into the consumer need you have identified? Sometimes new products or technologies will be needed, but more often than not, if you really adopt a "scarcity mentality," you may come up with many new ideas that could give new legs to your current product.

LESSON 67:
Play it by the numbers—Harness the power of claims

The use of claims that sound too good to be true is a bane of marketers the world over. Someone once told me that in a study of how credible different professions are perceived to be, marketers ranked right near the bottom, just above car salesmen. So when consumers see claims like "see the difference in one use/day/wash/week" or "money back guaranteed," they tend to tune out, dismissing the claims as marketing hype. This is unfortunate, as it paints a negative picture of an area of marketing that can really unleash a brand, if used properly. The problem is that haphazard, and sometimes unethical, use of claims has made this approach frowned upon. Used properly, claims can be one of the best weapons in your arsenal when it comes to driving growth. So what does "proper" use of claims entail?

1. First of all, be clear on the marketing objective. Is it increasing awareness, driving deeper trial or generating increased consumption? Stay away from nice-sounding but ultimately meaningless objectives like "re-igniting excitement" on the brand. Instead, focus on the fundamental behavior change you want to bring about in your consumer. If you are after awareness, skip this lesson and go back to the chapters on positioning and promotion to figure out what message you want to leave with your consumer and how to get it across.

2. If you are after consumer trial, focus on the big barriers that are holding consumers back from trying your brand. Do they feel your brand is no better than what they are using? Are they worried about adverse effects? Once you understand the barrier, figure out how you can enhance your basic benefit with claims that tackle this barrier. For example, if the barrier is a fear among consumers that your brand will not deliver on what it promises, you could address this with a message like "money back guaranteed" or with an endorsement from a credible source.

3. If you are after consumption increases, once again, look to the barriers that prevent consumers from buying more of your brand on each occasion or from buying your brand more often. Claims promising results over time or with repeated usage could be something to consider.

4. The final thought is to ensure that the claims you are making are

above board. Make sure your product actually delivers, and that you can back up what you are claiming in a way the consumer can actually experience. This is not a game of cooking up claims that sound exciting, but about being clear on the consumer fundamentals you want to impact and using your consumer understanding to make your benefit more desirable. If you do not stay rooted in what your brand can actually deliver, you will eventually be punished, either by disappointing consumers and putting them off of your product or service, or by ending up in court with legal trouble. So do yourself and your brand a favor and do not mess around when it comes to claims.

LESSON 68:
When old is gold—Remember that marketers become bored much faster than consumers

I was recently introduced to a new piece of jargon: "consumer promiscuity." Intrigued by what consumers' sex lives may have to do with my brand's fortunes, I decided to stop scribbling poetry and listen to what this person was saying in a meeting. Turns out, he was referring to how consumers are less loyal than ever given the continuously increasing spread of choices, and that innovation has become critical as a result. Some parts of that may well be true, but I think there is an even greater threat to a brand: that of "marketer promiscuity," or the tendency of marketers to jump to the next big thing instead of building what the brand stands for as a whole. Unfortunately, what often happens is that the consumer is not bored of the brand proposition, but the marketing team may be. To be fair, this is also partly caused by the reward structure in most organizations, where people feel that it is "sexier" to work on launching new items than on developing existing propositions. Now having looked at how to harness the power of marketing innovation, here are some practical tips on how to build these lessons into everyday decision-making for your brand.

1. Whenever you test new products, also test your strongest existing ones. You may be surprised to find that consumers often prefer old products that have resonated well with them instead of new items. By testing regularly, you let the consumers tell you when they are bored of your existing offerings and want to move on to something new.

2. Plan and assess marketing innovations with the same rigor that you would apply to a new product launch. See how you can exploit the idea or claim in-store, determine what media choices you could make

to get the message out most effectively, and utilize all aspects of the marketing mix instead of just advertising. By doing so, you give marketing innovations as fair a chance of building your brand as a new item launch.

3. See how your team or organization can celebrate marketing innovations the same way as new product launches. At the end of the day, what makes it exciting is not the actual launching of a new product, but the thinking and planning that allow your brand to attract more users and grow your sales and market share.

Yet another "P" of marketing: Planning

When most people think of marketing, they think of product launches, new advertising campaigns, and competitive moves and countermoves—in other words, a lot of the "here and now." No question about it, most marketers, me included, are in marketing because of the thrill of seeing our plans come alive in the marketplace. However, one critical aspect that is less talked about, but is no less important in terms of becoming a skilled marketer, is planning. Over the last few chapters, we have looked at various aspects of bringing innovations to market, whether they take the form of new products or marketing innovations on existing items. This chapter is focused on how to ensure that your brand does not become a "one-hit wonder" and how to set it up for sustainable success.

Building a brand is not something you do in a month, a year or even a couple of years. It takes sustained effort, and the ability to think beyond just the short term. Planning, developing critical path schedules, and anticipating resource gaps and needs are not usually associated as core skills needed of a marketer. However, this is yet another example of how in the real world a marketer needs to be more of an entrepreneur than a marketing specialist. If your brand were your own enterprise with your own money invested in it, you would likely take a more long-term view than one fiscal year or the next big launch, and you would want to make sure that it continues to generate returns in the future.

LESSON 69:
Always have a pipeline of future ideas at the ready

If big ideas are the lifeblood of growing a brand, the best thing you as a marketer can do is to make sure you don't run out of big ideas. One of the symptoms of a brand in trouble is when the team working on it stumbles to answer a simple question like what ideas do they think their brand will be exploiting nine months or a year down the line. Having a longer-term outlook is important so you are not always scrambling for ideas. First, many breakthrough ideas need technologies or capabilities to be developed that are just not going to happen overnight. The lay observer sees the spectacular success behind the launch of the iPod, but not the huge amount of research that went into perfecting it. Second, with the growing number of large retailers, the retail sector is becoming increasingly consolidated and organized, and these players demand longer-term planning so they can adjust their stores and strategies. So how do you ensure your brand is never short of ideas?

The first step is to adopt a mindset that acknowledges the importance of long-term planning. Here is a rule of thumb to get you started on this. On a sheet of paper, mark down the next two years divided into monthly or quarterly periods, and then try to fill up the calendar with your best guess of what ideas your brand will be exploiting in each phase. Chances are you will struggle, especially the farther into the future you go, but this is a critical starting point in planning. It will tell you where your pipeline of ideas looks strong and where you have gaps, which you can then proceed to fill. Make this a "living" document, so that as your plans change or you get better ideas, you can modify it.

The second step is to have more ideas that you currently know how to execute. The reality of the marketplace is that not every idea will work out—some technologies may fail, the competitive landscape may change, or you may just decide it no longer makes sense. So as you fill up your planning calendar, make sure you have more ideas than you can easily accommodate, knowing that some of your current plans will not make it to market. This also forces you to always have a pipeline of ideas ready, beyond what your immediate short-term business needs may require.

LESSON 10:
It won't come out of thin air—Set goals and measure sufficiency of your ideas

Planning for your brand's sustained long-term growth is a bit like planning for retirement—it is essential to know at the start where you want to end up. This is why when you meet a financial advisor, the first question you will likely be asked is what your financial goals are. Without knowing what you are aiming for, there is no way to judge whether your current plans are good, bad or just plain wishful thinking. So when it comes to a long-term growth plan for your brand, you need to start with what the desired end point is. Setting goals is equal parts art and science—set them too high, and you may be setting yourself up for demoralization and failure, but set them too low, and you risk breeding complacency and not realizing the full potential of what you may have achieved.

The first thing to nail down is the planning time horizon—for most businesses and brands, I would say you should stick to three to five years. Anything shorter than that becomes too much of the "here and now." Anything much longer starts to lose relevance, as many of the people working on the brand might have moved on by then—accountability is a great motivator when it comes to setting realistic goals! In terms of setting the goal, I would advocate a few criteria:

1. Keep it simple and memorable. A goal of 97.5 million will never stick as much as a goal of 100 million. Never underestimate the power of round numbers.
2. Try to make it externally focused. Most marketers are intensely competitive people, and the thrill of winning over the competition is one of the things that keeps them going. So becoming number one is a no-brainer, and if it makes sense for your brand, go for it. If outright market dominance is far out of reach, find a segment where you could aspire for leadership.
3. Keep it real. A simple check is to benchmark your brand's historic growth rates and those of your competitors. If achieving the goal you are proposing requires growing at much higher rates than what has been possible in the past, you either need a reality check or a

compelling reason why you feel it is possible (e.g. entering new markets or segments).

Once you have a goal and your pipeline of ideas, the next aspect of planning is to continuously evaluate your future pipeline of ideas for its ability to let you reach your goal. Using market research to measure consumer appeal, benchmarking past launches, or reviewing what competitors have done with similar activities would give you some estimate. Laying out your calendar and then superimposing how big each idea is will help do two things: it will show if you have gaps in reaching your goal, and it will indicate which ideas are the biggest contributors to achieving it.

LESSON 71:
Less is more—Prioritize and focus on the few big ideas

Vilfredo Pareto was born in 1848 and led an eventful life. He ran unsuccessfully for office, had a huge collection of wines, collected over a dozen pet cats, was a master swordsman, and married a penniless Russian girl who later ran away after 12 years of marriage. Fascinating as his life was, what most economists and management students know him for is the axiom that has come to be known as Pareto's Law. It began as an observation that in any society, 20% of the people tend to own 80% of the wealth, but over time it has come to imply that in most fields of human endeavor, it is the few important things (the 20) that make a big difference (the 80). People have subsequently used the "80-20" rule in fields as diverse as organizational behavior, supply chain management and personal life management.

Pareto's Law applies just as well when it comes to marketing planning. Market experience across industries shows that most value is created by a small percentage of successful ideas, while the vast majority of them fail altogether or add very little value. To be a successful marketer, you need to develop the skill of being able to identify these potential blockbuster ideas early. You also must ensure that your resources can be focused to make these ideas even bigger instead of spreading your resources thin by chasing a whole host of much smaller ideas. Identify the top 20% of these ideas and determine what proportion of your extra sales they contribute. If they do not contribute a disproportionately large amount (not necessarily exactly 80%, but much more than their fair share numerically), you probably have a problem of too many small ideas. The next step is to look at each of the top 20% ideas and focus on how you could make them bigger. As you do so, actively weed out the smallest ideas, so that you have a strong pipeline of future ideas and the bulk of your added sales comes from a few big ideas, which you can rally your team, resources and your customers around.

We have talked about developing a strong idea, figuring out how to market it and putting a plan in place to appropriately price it, supported by the right product and a pipeline of ideas. Unfortunately, all of that effort can go to waste if you do not know how to make your offering available to your consumers. To do that, we need to understand some of the challenges that you as a marketer will face in dealing with the next "P" of marketing: place.

PLACE

The future is here. It's just not widely distributed yet.
- William Gibson

In many organizations, sales and marketing are considered two sides of the same coin, with marketers expected to go through some sales experience and vice versa. Even in organizations where marketing is a separate department, there is usually a lot of emphasis placed on ensuring marketers stay rooted in the realities of what happens in sales through internships in the sales department or frequent field visits. The intent is not to make a master salesperson out of the marketer, but to ensure that marketing strategies are not concocted in the vacuum of air-conditioned conference rooms and instead are rooted in the realities of where consumer purchase decisions are finally made—at the point of sale. Another reason for marketers to ensure that "place" remains an integral P in their lexicon is that ultimately, this is not something that is somehow for the "guy in sales" to figure out. The point of purchase is perhaps the most important point of interaction between your brand and your consumer, because this is where the consumer finally decides to choose your brand or not. All your smart strategies and great advertising can come undone if your brand is not available where your consumer shops, or if you lose out to competing brands at the point of purchase because of weak packaging or inadequate visibility. As a result, a working knowledge of the fundamentals of what it takes to win at the point of purchase is an essential part of any marketer's repertoire of skills, and can often mean the difference between success and failure in the marketplace.

Shopping is like speed dating: The critical role of packaging

While "place" encompasses the critical aspects of distribution and visibility at the point of sale, when it comes to the broader question of ensuring your brand wins at the point of purchase, there are some aspects that are up to marketers to develop and influence. One aspect that is especially critical is your brand's packaging, which essentially is the "face" of your brand and embodies all the equities your brand stands for. By packaging, I do not just mean the container or bottle for packaged goods, but the total experience that consumers get when they see your brand—the logo and the key visual identities.

Have you ever taken part in speed dating? I don't have any particular interest in your love life, but in many ways marketers should approach packaging development as one would approach speed dating. In speed dating, you meet a number of people in a very short span of time and have to decide which one you are interested in based on your first visual impression, whatever information you can gather in the limited time you have together, and any signals that mark a person out as potentially being a good fit with you, such as shared interests, values, etc. Sounds eerily similar to browsing for products on a supermarket shelf, doesn't it? So put on some romantic music, get yourself in the mood, and join me as we seek the answers to developing great packaging in the world of speed dating.

LESSON 12:
Turning heads—Use packaging to stand out in the clutter

When you enter a room full of people of the opposite sex and you have just a few minutes with each one to decide whom you would like to know better, what would you do? According to research conducted on speed dating, the average person takes about eight minutes to decide whether someone is suitable as a potential mate or not. What the factors are in that decision is less certain. Some say it is the "smell" a person gives off, while others say it is the first visual impression. But one thing is certain: what counts in speed dating is making the right first impression. That is precisely the role your packaging plays in getting the consumers' attention when they step into the store. In many categories and markets, most consumers choose the brand they will buy only when they are in the shop, and in-store factors like packaging can play a huge role in swinging their decision. Your packaging must be able to stand out from all the other brands in the clutter and make the consumer stop and look. It sounds simple enough, but when you consider the proliferation of brands in most categories and that the consumer will spend at most a few seconds to scan all the brands in your category, it is quite a challenge. Getting it right involves a lot more than I could hope to cram into a couple of pages, but here are some things to consider:

1. Do you understand the visual cues that consumers expect of your category? Having some core category-related cues is a great starting point. For example, if you were selling baby products, a safe assumption would be that having a baby on the pack would give your brand a head start. However, it is not always that obvious, so find out what visual cues consumers consider essential, be they colors, visuals or other properties.

2. Make a clear choice on what core equities you want to drive on your packaging. As with positioning, your brand cannot embody every design element possible, so the more differentiated your packaging, the more you will communicate your brand's specific attributes as compared with the category's generic attributes.

3. Is your packaging clear in establishing who you are? Often, marketers agonize over the fine print, ignoring the fact that when looking at the packaging from a distance, what should really matter is clear and identifiable branding.

LESSON 13:
Learn the importance of "browser friendly" packs

Once that critical first impression has been made, you will probably not advance your love life much if you just stand there gawking. So what do you do? Simple: you engage in conversation to learn a bit about the other person and let the other person know more about you. It is a delicate balancing act, isn't it? Hold back too much and you risk being seen as aloof or not interested, but if you share too much too early, you risk being seen as coming on too strong.

When you are looking at your brand's packaging, there is a similar tightrope that you need to walk. In the context of speed dating, how much and what you choose to share depends to a large extent on what you make of the other person. Is he being open and sharing a lot? Does she seem genuinely interested in knowing more about you? Such insights into your consumer are the best place to start when you are wondering what kind of "conversation" you want your packaging to have with your consumer.

1. Understand how consumers in your category interact with packaging. Do they spend time reading what is on the back panel or do they just buy based on what is shown on the front? Do they want to know what ingredients are in the brand? If they pick up packs of different brands, what do they compare? This will help you understand what basic information you need to have on your pack and how to present it.

2. Be clear on what "marketing" you want to do via the text on your packaging. A common folly is to use the pack as a medium for writing an essay on everything your brand can offer. As with advertising in any other medium, choose carefully the one message you want your consumer to take away in the few seconds that they interact with your pack. With all the legal requirements you will need to fulfill, the space available for any "sell copy" will likely be precious—be selective in deciding what you use it for.

3. Is explaining how to use your product important? If it is, as may be the case with a new or less developed category or with a new technology,

by all means explain it—ideally in a visual way if possible. However, if your category is widely used and consumers know very well what to do with the product, save the space on your pack by omitting directions on its use.

LESSON 74:
You had me at hello—Use on-pack claims to close the sale

You and I may not have the charm or way with words that Tom Cruise did in his role as Jerry Maguire, but the ability to say the right words at the right time is a critical skill that everybody who has been in a relationship can appreciate. In the context of speed dating, given the immense time crunch you are under, this becomes even more critical. Lesson 73 was largely about getting the basics right and knowing what to include in a conversation. This will ensure that you are not an immediate turn-off, but if you really want to dazzle your consumer and hook them with your very first word, there is one trick you should have up your sleeve. That is the power of putting the right claims on packaging.

We have talked about how powerful claims can be in busting consumer barriers to your brand. Their use on packaging serves a similar purpose. The key difference is to use them in the right context—at the point of purchase. You need to understand what may hold the consumer back from choosing your brand at this critical decision point, or conversely, what added information could tip the scales in your brand's favor. The way you do it will largely depend on the specific dynamics of your category and consumer, but here are some common factors to consider:

1. Is there a specific product feature you want to draw attention to that may close the sale? For example, is there something that will prompt consumers to flip open the cap and smell a great new fragrance, or is there an improvement in performance that you want to remind them of?
2. Would providing reassurance of performance help? In Lesson 6 we talked about the concept of risk minimization, and if that is important for you, putting claims that help bust this barrier (for example, endorsements from credible sources or money-back guarantee claims) on the pack can be a great way to close the sale at the point of purchase.
3. If you can claim some superiority over your competition, this would be a good time and place to remind your consumer. The point of purchase is where your consumer will see competitive offerings side-

by-side, but all of your advertising on how your brand is better will be wasted if the consumer can't remember it at this crucial point. My advice: do not rely on luck or your consumer's memory. If you can claim superiority, try to communicate it at the point of purchase. There will often be space or other constraints on what you can put on your pack, but that is where you need to get creative—use stickers, merchandising materials or in-store aids to ensure that the message gets across at the point of purchase.

Size does matter: The role that big customers play today

It used to be that dealing with customers or retailers was something the "sales guys" had to worry about, and the marketer would only see them perhaps during field visits or sales conferences. "Retailers" was a term used to refer to a whole mass of customers, each of whom individually played a very small role in determining a brand's fortunes. That has long changed in many markets, and will almost certainly change in most markets in the years to come. The big driver of that change has been the emergence of giant customers, who have transformed several markets into oligopolies where a handful of retailers can determine a brand's fortunes. In many cases, they have unprecedented bargaining power. A classic example is Wal-Mart, which with a turnover of over $300 billion, dwarfs the manufacturers that supply it. As a result, getting your brand or a new product distributed into a major retailer is something that cannot be taken for granted, and the kind of support your brand gets instore can vary widely depending on what the retailer sees in your offer versus competitive offerings. This paradigm shift means that while you do not need to suddenly become a master of sales, as a marketer, you do need to know some of the basics of how to operate in such an environment.

LESSON 15:
Show me the money—Know that customers need to make money as well

I am a firm believer that to work well with someone, nothing beats empathy. No matter how different from you or how opposed to your point of view, making a genuine attempt to understand someone can work wonders. When I work with any new stakeholder—an agency, a direct report or a supplier—one of the first things I do is to transparently lay out what success looks like for me, and try and understand what it looks like for them. With that on the table, even if there are differences of opinion, we at least know what is driving our behavior and can thus address the issues. As manufacturers, when it comes to understanding retailers, a similar approach can be helpful—put yourself in their shoes and see what they are looking for.

The answer is actually quite simple: they are businesspeople and want what every other businessperson wants—profit maximization. So if you hear someone groaning about a retailer trying to gouge more money from your company or about how they are supporting a competitor who is throwing more money at them, why shouldn't they? If you were in their shoes, you would be trying to get the best financial deal from your suppliers as well. The key to success is to accept this reality, and instead of griping about it, try to figure out how you can use this understanding to win with your brand.

You don't necessarily have to just offer higher margins, as simple as that solution seems—you could keep increasing trade margins, but remember that you need to make money on your brand as well! To make this balancing act work, establish clearly what role your brand can play in the portfolio of brands (including those of competitive manufacturers) in terms of helping the retailers meet their objective of profit maximization. In general, if your brand has a high market share, you could exist with a lower than average margin. But if you have a smaller brand, you will need to provide a compelling story on how your brand brings in higher than average profitability per transaction to get retailer support. This sounds similar to how you would look at a portfolio of brands, doesn't it? This kind of thinking can ensure you get what you want for your brand and help you add value as a supplier that is not just looking at boosting its own gains, but is genuinely working toward a win-win solution.

LESSON 16:
Grow the category, don't just trade shares to win with the customer

The last lesson was about reconciling the profit maximization objectives of the manufacturer and the retailer. Another instance where there may be a conflict between what you as a marketer want and what a big retailer wants is the question of market shares. Most marketers swear by market shares as the ultimate barometer of their success, and that of their brands. Internal company sales goals are fine and good, but growing market shares is the purest measure of your brand's success in a competitive context. Growing market shares is also what marketers often use as an internal objective to rally their teams. As a result, in many organizations, marketers wait with bated breath every month to see how their brands have fared in the market share sweepstakes.

Hence, it seems natural for marketers to talk of their objectives in terms of share growth. Imagine their shock when they learn that customers actually do not give a damn how much share their brand gains! The reason for this lies in what we learned in the last lesson—as a retailer handling a portfolio of brands, seeing one of them go up at another's expense does not necessarily cause me any joy unless it helps me make more money overall. The answer for the marketer is not to abandon the quest for market share growth, but to reframe it in a way that makes it a win-win solution for the marketer and the customer. In general, there are two approaches you can take. If your brand is a premium-priced one, the argument can be simple: for every consumer who shifts to your brand from a lower-priced competitor, you increase category value and profits per transaction. The gains to the customer are clear, as is the case for why they should support your brand in-store. If your brand is lower-priced, the approach can be to prove that with its greater mass appeal, you can actually get more consumers into the category, thus increasing total category size and profits, even though your profit per transaction may be lower than that of premium brands.

If your brand does not fit easily into either category, then you need to do some hard thinking, as your brand may not have a clear role to play in the retailer's category game plan. In that case, proving that your brand taps into a unique segment of consumers that others cannot reach could be a useful approach. Whatever the case, what is clear is that dealing with customers is not just "sales work." When it comes to large customers with strong bargaining power, a lot of it comes down to the fundamentals of how your brand is positioned in the category—an area where the marketer can, and should, add value.

LESSON 11:
All in the family—Dealing with the trend of house brands

An emerging reality a marketer will have to confront in an environment where large retailers are an important part of your business is that they may become your competitors in addition to being the channel through which your brand reaches your end consumer. This is due to the growing trend among large retailers of launching "house brands," which are shelved alongside brands that they have traditionally carried. There are several reasons for this, one of which is the desire of large retailers to forward integrate and create more value for themselves. For marketers, it is just another pain in the neck. In addition to all the competition you had to deal with before, now you face yet another competitor, and this one belongs to the same customer whom you are relying on get your brand to the consumer!

The first thing to do is to recognize what the retailer is trying to do with the house brand. Yes, it is trying to make more money if possible, but unlike your other competitors, it is not really "out to get you." A retailer wants to grow the pie, not just have brands trade shares, and sometimes a house brand may be a way to get shoppers into a category by offering great value. Also, having a house brand can be an excellent negotiating tool for a retailer—in effect he can say to a manufacturer, "If your brand does not meet my margin and other needs, it is not indispensable for me to serve shoppers in the category." If you can present a coherent story on what role your brand will play in driving category sales and profits for the retailer, you have little to worry about. Where brands often stumble is when they seem to have no unique reason to exist from a customer standpoint vis-à-vis its house brand—that is when you get into ugly conversations about customers not wanting to shelve or support your brand.

The second piece of advice I would offer is to not underestimate house brands. Often they are dismissed as "no name" brands, but remember that they do bring a strong equity to the table—that of the customer. Furthermore, large customers often have a lot of expertise in understanding shopper behavior that may go into the creation and support of these brands, reliant as they often are on in-store support. As such, you may be able to learn something new about your category from these house brands.

The final frontier: Winning in small stores and developing markets

One of the things I like about marketing is the diversity of experiences that you get in learning to cope with varied consumer and customer environments. So while the last chapter was about mega customers with scale sometimes dwarfing manufacturers, this one is about small stores that dot the landscape of so many developing markets. Insignificant by themselves in terms of the impact they have on a brand's sales, and sometimes no more than the proverbial hole in the wall, collectively these stores hold the key to the fortunes of billion-dollar corporations in their quest to tap into the emerging economies and consumers of the developing world. The recent hype about India and China aside, the phenomenon of seeking faster growth by tapping into developing markets is something many multinationals have embraced for years. With their recently opened, faster growing economies, young populations and growing middle classes, they have been an irresistible lure for multinationals. However, many globally successful brands have stumbled in tapping into these markets, in part due to inadequate consumer understanding, and often in large part due to the very different retail environment—one usually dominated not by a few large customers as in some Western markets, but by literally millions of small stores, often scattered over large geographical areas. This environment throws up some unique challenges to the marketer.

LESSON 18:
Chicken or egg? The dilemma of sales and distribution in small stores

In an environment where large customers dominate, the equation is relatively straightforward: sell your brands to the retailers and once you gain distribution in their stores, consumer pull will kick in. In many developing markets where small stores predominate, the equation can sometimes be turned on its head. Marketers are left tearing their hair out in frustration that they are not able to get enough distribution for their brands, which is restricting their consumer pull. The reality of getting distribution in small stores is a very different challenge, and it is something that the marketer may not directly influence. One key difference that has direct impact on marketing is that in the small stores that dominate so many developing markets, consumer pull is often a critical pre-condition for getting deeper distribution, not the other way around. How does that happen, and what could that mean for your marketing plan?

The first consideration is to see life through the eyes of the small retailers. Yes, they are businesspeople just like the largest customer in the most developed market, but there are some critical differences. The small retailer is likely to have much smaller retail space available, much less capital to tie up in inventory, and much lower access to institutional funding. As a result of all these constraints, small store owners can usually keep only a few brands or items from any category, and generally tends to focus on the best-selling ones. This makes the retailers relatively risk averse in terms of stocking new items, unless they are confident that the new products will sell well with their shoppers. Added to this is the fact that your sales team may not even directly cover many of these stores. As a result, you end up relying on these store owners taking the initiative to buy your brand from the wholesale channel or redistributors.

The second factor is to understand how shopping behavior in small stores differs from large stores. The retail environment sometimes does not allow self-selection, or at best allows limited browsing opportunity. As a result, consumers often decide on the brand to buy before they come to the store, and ask the retailer to give them the brand of choice.

The combination of these two factors means that the best barometer for the small storeowners of whether a brand will sell is consumers coming and asking them for it. The practical implication for your marketing plan is that you should not wait for distribution before your demand generation plans kick in. Instead, start your marketing and advertising in parallel, or often even before your sales team goes out to try placing your brand in stores.

LESSON 19:
The 10-foot rule to in-store visibility

It is an old marketing axiom that when it comes to any in-store environment, what is visible sells. The importance of securing strong in-store visibility is even more critical in a small-store environment. This is because these stores are often cluttered, rarely have the shelves sorted neatly by category as they are in bigger stores, and, in some cases, have no concept of shelving at all when it comes to streamers of sachets hanging together from a wire on the ceiling, as found in many stores in developing markets. Where a lot of multinationals and even a lot of local companies fail is in ensuring that their brand is visible in a way that works for this environment at the point of purchase. A lot of this comes down to the people involved. Though it is unfair to generalize, a lot of them come from considerably different backgrounds compared to consumers who shop at these small stores, and they may not be accustomed to shopping in such an environment. As a result, a lot of their thinking and how they look at in-store material is from the point of view of someone shopping in a supermarket or large store. The material they create may thus work well as a print ad or in a large store, but may be a total dud in a small-store environment. It is not that the material is good or bad *per se*, just that it may be out of sync with the shopping realities for the small-store consumer in a developing market. These are the types of insights you as a marketer need to bring to the table in developing in-store materials.

As a rule of thumb, I recommend that when evaluating any material you are considering putting up in a small store, take several steps back, and look at it from at least 10 feet away. Then see what is visible and what is not, since this is how your consumer will likely see your material. The key is to recognize that in such stores, shoppers are rarely as close to the material as they are in a large store. In many cases, they are viewing the material from several feet away, and in poor lighting conditions. As a result, it is important to focus on simplicity and clear visibility when it comes to communication. Forget about small text with fancy claims that someone needs to be a few inches away to read. Focus on the basics:

1. Clearly establish your brand.
2. Establish the specific item you are offering.
3. Convey your benefit in as visual and as simple a way as possible.

LESSON 80:
Big things come in small packages—Use the power of sizing and pricing

Even if you have the right consumer understanding and managed to get the right proposition for your brand, there is one additional factor that can make or break your brand in developing markets. That is the power of getting your sizing and pricing right for these consumers. Making the right proposition available at the right cash outlay has often been the tipping point that has exploded categories and brands in developing markets. This does not mean selling watered-down products at cheap prices, but rather figuring out the right price points and launching products in the right sizes. In many categories, offering products in small bottles, sachets or portions at lower price points has been the spark that has enabled the categories to take off. There are some clear reasons for this. Many of these categories tend to have a far lower level of development or penetration than in more developed markets, hence consumers may not be willing to pay a higher outlay for a larger size. Also, the realities of lower average incomes in developing markets may mean that a smaller size with a lower price point is necessary to maintain the same price-to-income ratio as is offered to consumers in more developed markets.

So how do you go about determining the ideal size and price? If there are existing brands in the category, you can benchmark based on what other brands are doing, especially market leaders or brands driving growth in trial in the category. Then, depending on your desired pricing strategy, you slot your brand in. It is much trickier when there are few or no existing brands in your category. The following questions may get you started on thinking about what the right trial size and price are for your brand:

1. What is the lowest dosage or consumption that would allow consumers to fully experience the benefit that your brand or category offers? That

could be a good starting point in determining the minimum amount you need to provide per "shot."

2. What are the dynamics of coinage and pricing in the market beyond your category? It may sound silly, but the amount people pay for everyday things like an egg or a cigarette can often be good benchmarks for what could be a good trial price point. We talked a bit about determining possible "magic" price points in the chapter on pricing, and putting this together with the answers to the previous question can get you some concrete options on sizing and pricing.

A slightly different ball game: The challenges of marketing to the shopper

With the growth of large retailers, and the growing importance of the consumer experience at the point of purchase in determining brand choice, life has changed for the marketer in a fundamental way: the emergence of the point of purchase as another medium to drive consumer preference. Gone are the days when marketers could develop advertising, put it on air, and wait for consumers to buy their brand. With the growing importance of what happens in-store, it is almost as if the in-store environment has evolved from something the sales force would deal with to another media choice for marketers deciding how to influence their consumer. This brings with it a new challenge: figuring out how to market to the shopper. It may seem obvious—use all the same principles that you would use in any other medium. To an extent this is true, but what makes it interesting is that the person who shops for your brand may well be different from the person who consumes it. Even if it is the same person, the kind of information the consumer looks for in-store and the factors that swing the brand preference at the point of purchase can often be very different.

Mother knows best, or does she? Learn who shops, who consumes and who influences

When I was a kid, my dad and I were pretty clueless about what brands were being brought into the household in most categories—it was something mom would figure out and do. Indeed, in a lot of categories, especially those related to household products and services, the stereotype is that it is the "female head of the household" or the "homemaker" who decides on the brands and who does the shopping. This is why a lot of marketing in these categories has traditionally targeted women, and why in so much marketing literature, the consumer is inevitably referred to as "she." While that has not entirely changed, there are some fundamental shifts that a marketer needs to consider in figuring out how to market to the shoppers of today.

First and foremost, with the rise of dual income families and increasing numbers of women in the full-time workforce, the job of shopping for the family is no longer purely a female preserve. Secondly, with growing fragmentation and sophistication in most categories, there is rarely anything as monolithic as the "family's choice." Finally, with the earlier age at which kids nowadays seem to be exposed to media— whether through advertising or the Internet—the importance of children as influencers in several categories has increased. As a marketer, you are probably familiar with the type of person who actually consumes your brand, but to get started on marketing to the shopper, you need to be very clear on who fills two distinct roles in the purchase decision: the shopper and the influencer.

While the principles of developing communication for the shopper and the end consumer are the same (create a single-minded proposition, tackle their barriers to trying your brand, etc), if the shopper is someone different from the end consumer, then the message you need to use at the point of purchase will need to tackle different barriers. As an example, the kids in the household may be the ones actually consuming breakfast cereals, but the mother may be doing the shopping, with very different questions on her mind ("How healthy is this?") than the kids ("Does it have chocolate?"). Understanding who the influencers are and their role in the purchase decision is also something that could prove invaluable. In the example above, putting claims about how healthy your cereal is on the pack could convince the mom to pick it up, but including some desirable freebies like toys in the box could ensure that the kids pester her to choose it again.

What I learned shopping for beer—Use the power of adjacencies

Years ago, my friends and I used to buy beer from a small store in our neighborhood. Often, when we were late coming home from work or were simply feeling lazy, we would call the store and ask for delivery to our apartment. A constant source of frustration was that the store did not sell any chips, nuts or other snacks that we liked to enjoy with our beer. So we would have to go to another store to pick these up. The thought often struck me that it was a missed business opportunity for the liquor store—it could have had some easy added sales and some delighted customers if it stocked even a basic assortment of snacks. The store did not understand the need it was satisfying. My friends and I wanted to spend an evening chilling out, which required more than just beer—we needed snacks, and come to think of it, music as well. Understanding what need you are satisfying could be the factor that tips the scales in favor of your brand at the point of purchase when it comes to attracting the shopper. Ask yourself what other products or services your consumer might use in conjunction with your brand, such as the beer and chips example. With this understanding, you could impact the point of purchase in a number of ways—from ensuring your brand is displayed and shelved near these "adjacent" products to potentially doing promotions with such products to drive trial of your brand. Done systematically, this could go well beyond tactical promotions and enable your brand to own some consumption occasions in the consumer's mind, which could be a source of competitive advantage. An example is the effort put in by Tiger Beer to own the "enjoying the Soccer World Cup with friends" position, which encompassed giveaways with World Cup team logos included with the beer, contests and promotions around the World Cup theme, and advertising that celebrated this occasion.

Seeing is believing—Use the power of in-store demonstrations

I have often wondered how many people really buy products because they are advertised on TV shopping networks, given how most of the spots seem so long-winded and over the top. What a lot of brands try to squeeze into 30-second commercials, these spots seem to relish in taking tens of minutes or more to communicate. For all their faults, they do have one thing going for them: almost all of them feature a "live" demonstration of the product, whether it is a juicer transforming large fruits to pulp instantly or a grill churning out perfect steaks without excess oil. I am sure every marketer would love to do a similar demonstration, but unless Santa Claus brings a magically enhanced media budget this Christmas, this is not likely to happen.

While you may never be able to do a drawn-out demonstration in your TV spots, there is another medium where this is a more realistic possibility, and that is in-store. We discussed earlier how the point of purchase is increasingly emerging as another medium for your brand to interact with the consumer and for you to influence brand choice. We have identified a lot of things you could do to influence this point of interaction, but one of the most important things you could do is showcase your brand's benefits live at the point of purchase. Not every category and every brand will have a benefit that lends itself to a live demonstration, but if yours does, you need to dive in without further thought. One of the most common trial barriers across categories is credibility in claims that consumers see on TV, in part because the airwaves have become saturated with so many claims and so much puffery. The best way to bust that would be to show that your brand does actually deliver at the point where it matters most: the point of purchase.

We are almost in the home stretch now, and if you were to go by most conventional marketing books, we would have exhausted all the "P's" of marketing. However, in the real world, there is another "P" that in my opinion makes all the others fade into insignificance. If you want to succeed in the real world, or at least learn what makes it different from the world of marketing textbooks, you need to know this "P" well.

It is called "people."

PEOPLE

So much of what we call management consists in
making it difficult for people to work.

— Peter Drucker

You may be wondering what business I have starting a section entitled "People," given that I am by no stretch of the imagination a human resources (HR) professional nor do I have any academic qualifications in organizational behavior or HR. To be clear, I have no pretensions of being an expert in either field. However, what I do have is some real-world experience in understanding what it takes to translate marketing strategies and thinking into results. On this basis, I know enough to understand that to a large extent, success in the real world depends not just on how smart you are, but also on how well you can work with others, whether it is your agency, your management or other departments. In general, being an ogre when it comes to dealing with people is a recipe for disaster in the real-world workplace, no matter how smart you happen to be or where you earned your MBA. What makes it especially challenging for marketers is that to deliver results, they must depend on others to some extent. The other aspect of this "P" is the person at the center of it all: the marketer. Marketing is at best an inexact science, and a lot of the results you get out of it depend on your motivations and skills.

Does familiarity breed contempt? The double edge of continuity

An important aspect of this often underestimated "P" of marketing is how you can develop your own marketing skills and ensure that they remain finely honed to help you cope with the various consumer, market and competitive contexts that are likely to be thrown your way in the course of a career in marketing.

As with any other aspect of life, practice makes perfect, and truly knowing a market or category can take a long time. The advantages of the continuity that comes with working on a brand or category for years is obvious—a thorough understanding of what makes the brand tick, developing an intuitive "gut feel" for what will or will not work, and a clear understanding of competition. If you were to look at it purely from the point of view of what it would take to build and grow a brand, you would want the same team members working on it forever, enabling them to keep using and building their expertise. However, looking at it as an individual managing your career, sticking with one brand forever does not work so well. While building expertise is fine and good, you do want career advancement, better prospects and diverse experiences. This chapter gives you some hints on how you could get the best of both worlds.

LESSON 84:
Build an area of expertise, don't be a jack of all trades

As marketers, we build our expertise in a number of areas that help us think through how we can create a differentiated positioning for a brand and then market it in a way that makes it attractive to the target consumers. The basic skills involved are essentially an ability to understand what people need and how you can set what you have to offer apart from competitors in the consumers' minds. However, what marketers do far less often is to apply some of this thinking to themselves as they build their careers in marketing. Whenever I talk to anyone about their career interests, or look at my own, I start with the question: If I were a brand, what would my distinctive positioning be? Just as a brand grows equity by sticking to a well-defined positioning, you stand to gain a lot in your career by defining what core skills, experiences or areas of expertise you bring to the table in a way that sets you apart from others. So whenever the question of continuity versus seeking diverse experiences comes up, or when the temptation of a career move for short-term benefits comes up, this is a thought that could keep you focused on how you could build your career.

By all means you should seek out new experiences or better prospects, but as you build your career, keep asking yourself what unique positioning you are creating for yourself. It could be experience on a brand or category, in a particular market, or in marketing to a particular consumer segment (e.g. children). It is sometimes difficult to think this through as you begin your career, so do not agonize too much if you cannot answer it early on. When I started working, I had no idea where I was headed and would not have bet too much money on continuing to work in the corporate sector for more than a couple of years. However, as you encounter different consumer, market and competitive contexts, you will begin to get a feel for what you enjoy and seem to do well at. There is also the element of chance, as you will not always be able to control what assignment you end up doing. But between this understanding of what you seem to be good at and the experiences you pick up along the way, you should after a couple of years of working have a good idea of the area in which you want to start building your positioning as a "brand."

LESSON 85:

Those who forget history are condemned to repeat it—Know the heritage and history of your brand

Marketers are only human, and some basic human traits that come to the fore in marketing are the tendency to believe that one can do better than what has been done before and the desire to leave one's mark on the brand. As a result, every time a brand gets a new brand manager, it is a safe bet that a strategy overhaul is in the cards. This is not necessarily a bad thing, as fresh thinking and perspective almost always help, no matter how well the brand is doing. However, where it becomes potentially suicidal is when it leads to constantly reinventing the wheel and repeating mistakes that have been made before. I hate jargon and buzzwords, but one that I do like is "360 degree marketing," though my definition of this phrase is slightly different from what the marketing gurus may have intended. To me it means that if you wait long enough and change enough brand managers, you will always come back to where you started!

The way out of this trap is relatively simple—all you need is the humility to learn from what has been done before on your brand and accept that there is no shame in reapplying some of this instead of trying to reinvent everything. I am not saying you should just repeat everything that has been done before—by all means innovate and change, but do develop a thorough understanding of what has previously worked or not worked for your brand. Nothing beats knowledge, and combining deep knowledge of the past with innovation could give you the edge that you and your brand need. Some thoughts on how you could do this:

1. Map the growth history and chart the share or sales progress of your brand over the last few years, and overlay on this all aspects of the marketing mix that are relevant to your brand—the launches, media spending, distribution, pricing moves, etc. Then identify the periods when your brand had the strongest growth and the slowest growth, or declined. Once you have done this, look for the connections and see what kinds of ideas and what marketing plan elements have been correlated with growth or decline.

2. Repeat this exercise for your key competitors to develop a better understanding of what makes them tick.

3. Once you have built this knowledge, always keep it handy so you can use it to develop future plans by replicating past success elements and also to ensure you do not repeat past blunders.

LESSON 86:
Passing the baton—Ensure knowledge continues even if people do not

You may have built up all the knowledge to make you a master of your brand, but it is inevitable that one day you will move on. Perhaps you will change jobs, perhaps you will move to another assignment in the same company, or perhaps you will do what I often fantasize about doing— retire, write books and sip cocktails on the beach. Whatever the reason, one of the responsibilities of a brand manager is not just to grow the brand while you are running it, but to set up the brand for sustainable success in the future.

A big part of doing that lies in ensuring continuity of knowledge. If you do a good enough job of capturing and documenting what works and does not work on your brand, your successor will have a much easier time, and you will not have to worry about all your hard work coming undone because the new guy repeats some mistakes of the past. I have seen people do it in many ways—it could be a fancy booklet, print-outs or a PowerPoint presentation that documents as much information on the brand as possible so that if you were to disappear tomorrow, people could still run the brand seamlessly.

It is tough to wake up one day and decide to distill years of learning in a few days or hours. If nothing else, the sheer work involved will be a big turn off, especially if you are also worried about moving on to your new job or assignment. My practical suggestion would be to do this exercise on an annual basis, capturing all the lessons as the year draws to a close. This needs to go beyond just a report card that many organizations compile to include some of the more fundamental success factors. Such an annual compilation of lessons has two benefits. First, you keep refreshing your knowledge, and that of your team, on what is working and not working on your brand, which you can then apply to your plans. Second, when it is time to move on, you can pass them on to your successor as the best possible welcome gift!

It takes two to tango: Forming winning agency partnerships

When I was in business school, I literally fell in love with advertising. I took all the courses available, read everything I could lay my hands on, and did some freelance projects for local firms (which had the added benefit of paying for much junk food and beer). Having long been interested in writing, the parallels with advertising development—of creating something new and seeing it come to life in print or on TV—really stoked this passion. After I started working came the realization that in the real world of marketing, developing advertising is not that simple. As a marketer, you may have the initial idea or craft the strategy, but to translate this into advertising, you need to work with an indispensable ally: your advertising agency. From coming up with a provocative creative idea to translating it into superb execution, your advertising strategies will not progress beyond internal memos unless your agency is up to the task. One of the most critical skills you will need to succeed as a marketer is the ability to get the best possible work out of your agency.

LESSON 81:
Swapping shoes—Understand what makes them tick

On first sight, agency people can look like another species to novice marketers. The account people may look similar to marketers, but they are always in a panic about timelines and billings, and it is not always clear why they keep trying to question the strategies on your brand (to any agency people reading this, I am exaggerating to make a point). The creatives may seem a breed apart, looking, talking and acting differently from the account people. I mentioned earlier that when in doubt, bank on empathy, and this is no exception. Instead of giving platitudes about understanding them better, I will share a tip you could use tomorrow: spend a day doing an exercise called Swapping Shoes. Take any project you are working on and reverse the roles. Let the marketing team act as the agency and the agency team act as the clients, going through all the meetings and activities they would in a normal day, and then meeting at night over dinner or beer to share what they learned. It is fun, but more importantly, it will give you some insights into what makes your agency partners tick and give them an understanding of what your life is like. What you learn will depend on your specific situation and the people involved, but here are some observations I have picked up:

1. Your brand is not just "your" brand. Your agency partners feel as much ownership and passion for it as you do, and they are also rewarded for its success. So instead of treating them like hired help or contractors, think of them as a part of your team like any other department in your organization.

2. For creatives, it is not just business—it is personal. When you create anything, you are investing a lot of yourself into it, and sharing it with others is a nerve-wracking experience (just ask any writer who has waded through rejection slips). Use this understanding to avoid rejecting their work in the same impersonal way you might a pricing proposal. Respect their creativity. If you like their work, celebrate together; if you do not, explain why it does not meet your business needs, but do not pass judgment on their creativity in general.

3. The account people want to contribute to strategy not because they are out to take your job, but because they want to add value and not be seen as messenger boys between the client and the creatives. Remember they can add a lot of value. Not only are they often as qualified as many folks in your marketing team, they also bring the

benefit of working across brands, which allows them to bring a totally new perspective to your business.

4. Account people fuss about billing because they should. If you were running your own business, would you not want your customers to pay you on time? It is not "sexy" work, but help them manage this and make sure this is not a pain for them.

LESSON 88:
Learn your agency's true value—It can do much more than just advertising

In many ways, a good advertising agency can be the most important resource in helping a marketer succeed. The obvious contribution is to develop advertising that brings your strategies to life for your consumers. However, you can get much more value from a strong agency partnership, if you know what to look for.

One instance is when your agency has people who have been working on your brand for a long time, much longer than you have been around. If you are lucky enough to have someone from the agency's creative side who has spent a long time working on your brand, you have a goldmine on your hands. You could get insights into what worked and failed beyond what you could learn from any internal memo, and without any "wallpaper" to make things look rosier than they may have been—a common feature when you ask your predecessors what they did wrong! All you need to do is to be willing to have a chat, and yes, offering to buy the beer does not hurt.

Your agency can also be a great sounding board for ideas on your brand, especially if they are unpopular or new ideas for your team. This is because the agency will understand your brand and business but will not care about the internal politics in your organization, and will not have any "agenda" that may prevent you from having an objective discussion. For example, an idea to cut prices may put your company's finance guy up in arms about profits, while an idea to cut product costs could prompt R&D to start listing all of the reasons why the money is needed. Your agency will not care, and could help you think through the pros and cons and challenge your thinking in a more objective manner. Your agency is a resource and you can bounce ideas and find help in developing your plans, even if they have nothing to do with advertising. All you need to do is ask.

LESSON 89:
Sugarcoating is for candies—Tell it as it is, and you will earn respect

When you are the new kid on the block, working with agencies can be a scary experience, especially when you need to start giving feedback on ideas or advertising being proposed for your brand. First of all, you do not want to screw up in front of them or your bosses, saying you love something only to have your boss dismiss it as a piece of junk. There is also the fear of damaging your relationship with the agency by criticizing the work too harshly if you do not like it. Then again, there is the tendency in too many organizations to be irritatingly politically correct. As a result of these conflicting forces, agencies are sometimes left totally confused by what they hear from young marketers.

A typical feedback session could start with gushing but largely meaningless comments ("I love where you're taking this," "I'm so excited that we are meeting on this project"), followed by a litany of things the marketers like and do not like. The problem is that your agency does not want an analysis of all the pros and cons—more than anything else, it just wants to know whether or not you will buy the work. The agency may not like it if you do not buy the work, but it will respect you for having a point of view and not just mumbling some platitudes and waiting for your boss to make the call. Here are some suggestions on how to share your feedback on creative work proposed by your agency:

1. First of all, take the time to understand what is being proposed. This is not an exam where people are looking to you for the "right" answer, so do not become stressed, ask all the questions you want, and clarify any doubts before you jump in with your decision. This also makes the agency feel like you are genuinely seeking to understand instead of rushing to judgment.
2. Say clearly whether the work meets your needs or not. As mentioned, you are not there to pass judgment on whether the work is good or bad, but to see if it works for your brand and business needs.
3. Then give a few directions on what could be improved if you do not buy the work as it is. In case you do want to buy it as it is, just say so—you don't have to nitpick.
4. See how you can make the atmosphere less stressful for all concerned. Presenting work to clients can be nerve-wracking for creatives, and marketers treating such meetings like an inquisition do not help. It

may sound simple, but try a trick like not sitting with the agency on one side of the table and your team on the other—mix it up so that it is not "us versus them," but rather one team trying to do the best for the brand you all work on.

View from the top: Managing management

When it comes to succeeding in the real world, one of the most critical factors will be how you manage your bosses. It is idealistic to think that you should just do all the right things and the rest will follow. It is rarely so simple when real people are involved. Here are some thoughts on how to succeed as a marketer, taking into account that there will be people more senior than you who also have a big stake in your brand, and may have ideas of their own on how to go about it.

LESSON 90:
Don't let there be a leadership void, or your boss will fill it

Put yourself in their shoes and see how the world looks from their standpoint. They are equally, if not more, responsible for your brand's success, but are not as close to the day-to-day operations as you are. They probably have a bunch of other headaches to sort through, and their own managers to manage, so life would be so much easier if they did not have to wade through every little detail. Also, their success is at least in part determined by whether you grow in your career or not and they would love it if you did well. So nirvana for any boss is a business that is under control and subordinates who can lead the thinking and take care of the details, which in turn makes the boss look good. On the other hand, a nightmare scenario is when the business is in deep trouble, the subordinates are clueless about what to do, and worst of all, the boss looks bad through no fault of his own. At times like that, a boss will start micro-managing the details and essentially doing your work. This is the kind of hellish situation you want to steer clear of.

The first thing you can do as a marketer to avoid such an "invasion" by your boss is to understand what does work or does not work for the success of your brand. Doing so will ensure that even if things go wrong, you will likely be the person who has the best idea of what to do, or at least have an understanding of what went wrong. In a tough situation, your boss must be confident that you are on top of things, and nothing works better to build that confidence than knowledge. The second thing you can do is to translate this knowledge into visible leadership. At a time like this, you cannot afford to have it appear that your brand is a ship without a captain, because then your boss will step in and take charge. To demonstrate that you have things under control, dip into the bag of tricks we discussed in the chapter on dealing with a business crisis.

LESSON 91:
The curious case of the Iraqi information minister—Share both good and bad news promptly to build credibility

It is human nature to look for the silver lining in anything—if nothing else, it makes us feel like we are more in control of our destinies than we may really be. Nothing has exemplified this in recent times more than the tragi-comic story of Mohammed Saeed al-Sahaf, Saddam Hussein's information minister. His press conferences and statements during the US invasion of Iraq in 2003 have become the stuff of legend, spawning websites, fan clubs, and DVDs showing the "best of al-Sahaf." The poor guy became a universal object of ridicule because of his insistence, often in colorful language, of the how the US forces were being slaughtered and beaten back, while in reality they were racing to Baghdad, sweeping aside the little resistance the Iraqi military put up. He continued until the very end, insisting victory was imminent when US tanks were in fact entering Baghdad.

You may never get the kind of notoriety that al-Sahaf did, but a sure way to lose all credibility with your management is to share only the good news and sweep the not-so-good news under the carpet. Sooner or later it will catch up with you, and you will have a disaster on your hands as far as your business and your career are concerned. Something I have seen countless times is that when there is the slightest piece of good news, whether it is an increase in market share or a launch getting off to a good start, people are lightning fast to share it all around. But when there is any bad news, it takes much longer for it to trickle up the chain. You may think you are succeeding in not looking bad, but your managers are not stupid—the bad news will reach them eventually, so you might as well be the first one to share it. There are just two things to remember. First, share bad news just as promptly as you would good news—that will mark you out as someone of integrity. Second, do not become simply a messenger—when there is bad news to share, offer your views on what could be done to fix it. Doing this will buy you the space you need to work things out without your manager stepping all over your toes.

LESSON 92:
Know how to take advice based on the four types of people you will meet

A common problem in any organization is that while money, people and other resources may be scarce, there is one thing that always seems to be in abundance: free advice from all sorts of people, many of whom may be senior to you. Even assuming that all the input you get is well intentioned and could help you, there is no way you will ever be able to please everyone. The answer is not to become so flexible that you lack any opinion, or to become a thick-skinned ogre who pisses everyone off by not listening to anyone. Decide what advice to take on and how to act on it based on who it is coming from. I have a theory that in any business decision, the people you meet are playing one of four roles:

1. The Decision Maker – This is the person or people who have the final decision power over what you are doing. It could be your boss or your boss' bosses, but what is obvious is that for this group, you not only need to take their inputs and opinions very seriously, but you also must ensure they know what you are thinking early on and that they remain engaged in what you want to do with your brand.

2. The Resources – These are the people whom you actually need to help you get the job done on your brand. A good example could be your agency. While it does not have veto power on decisions, taking the agency's inputs to heart early will ensure it is on board with you. Differences of opinion are bound to happen, and you will need to deal with them as you would in any other team situation. The key thing to remember is that if the team cannot agree, do not debate endlessly. Take the options available, give them to the Decision Maker, and get a decision and move on.

3. The Interested Stakeholders – These are the large group of people who may have some interest or stake in your results, but they cannot veto your plans and they are not actually needed to do the work. Some examples are people who have worked on your brand before and are always ready to share how they did things, or senior management who are not directly in your reporting line, like the sales director, but who still insist on commenting on your advertising. The key to managing this group's advice lies in attentive listening but selective action. Always be polite and hear them out. It is a small world, so why piss them off, and who knows, you may get some genuinely good ideas. However, remember that you are not bound to act on their advice; take on board what you find useful and dump the rest.

4. The Background Buzz – This is all the crap you hear in the hallways, around the coffee machine and over drinks on Friday evenings. It could be peers eager to show how smart they are by sharing gratuitous "insights" or the latest gossip from the office grapevine. My advice for dealing with these people is "in one ear and out the other!"

Bear in mind that these are roles, not individuals, and so the same person could play a different role in a different situation. As you get into any project or activity on your brand, it is important to have a clear idea of who is playing what role, and to act accordingly when it comes to all the advice and opinions you will inevitably be given.

No, they are not really all out to get you: Working with other departments

Everyone likes to gripe about how tough they have it, and marketers are no exception. If you hang around a group of marketers grumbling over beer after work, chances are the most common subjects will be, in no particular order, their bosses (but then, who does not complain about their boss?), their agencies and other functions or departments in the company. As a marketer you need a whole host of other departments to help you deliver what you need for your brand: the R&D folks to develop the right product, the finance department to help with pricing and managing the profits, the sales team to get your brand into stores, and so on. Whenever there are so many stakeholders, conflicts and differing opinions are to be expected. To the young marketer trying to work through the different political agendas, it can be quite frustrating and seem as if the other departments are conspiring against doing what is right for the brand.

LESSON 93:
Row together to move the boat forward—Understand what success means for them and make them part of the solution, not the problem

Yes, it's the "E" word again—empathy—try and understand what is at stake for the other side. When you are feeling frustrated, it's easy to think other departments are out to get you, but that kind of attitude will not make things any better. Before we go any further, you need to understand two basic truths if you are contemplating a career in marketing:

1. Marketing is not by any means more important than any other department. There is a common misconception that marketing is the only department trying to do what is right for the brand and everyone else somehow does not care about sales and is just trying to hold marketing back. If you disagree, you need help of the sort provided to those who believe little green men are out to get them.

2. In the real world you will not succeed without the other departments, no matter how brilliant your marketing, and you need all of them to be pulling together to succeed. If you hear the other departments complaining about marketers, the most common refrain will be that they are arrogant and do not value the other departments or involve them early enough.

So if moaning does not help and ignoring them is not an option, what do you do? Recognize that you need them on your side to succeed, and develop a plan to make that happen. It takes some work, but it will make your life much easier. Start with understanding what success means for each of them. In any organization, chances are that every department does have a strong stake in overall business success, but may measure success based on some specific, smaller subsets of it. Once you understand the different aspects, at the very least you will know where they are coming from and can thus plan for it. For example, if you are contemplating a pricing move on your brand, talking to the finance team members early and asking them what it may mean for profits would be a smart thing to do.

However, what you could do with this understanding is far beyond just this. When you start any project or activity, pull in all the departments at the very outset. Lay out what you are trying to do for the brand, and the business or competitive case. Ask for input on their area of expertise and understand how they would define success. You may not agree on everything, but they will feel a part of the solution, not the problem, and you will not be the pushy "marketing guy" but rather someone trying to rally everyone to drive your business forward.

LESSON 94:
Success has many fathers—Be generous in acknowledging others' contributions

For most companies, the most visible signs of success are measures like sales and market share. So it's not surprising that activities like new product launches and competitive responses in the marketplace that are visible contributors to these measures tend to hog a lot of the limelight. We have all heard of the "Cola Wars," the "Burger Wars" and so many other marketing "wars" that one could be forgiven for wearing a flak jacket to work. Add to that the "glamour factor" often associated with advertising, and you have the perfect recipe for marketing being disproportionately credited with a company or brand's success in the business press. Even within an organization, it is often the sales and marketing teams who have the "sexiest" news to share—whether it is new advertising, colorful photos of how a new launch looks in-store, or press conferences featuring top celebrities.

The net result of this is two-fold. First, it makes it tempting for marketers to start believing this myth of marketing indispensability. Second, even if the marketers do not let this go to their heads, it is easy to understand why other departments may be left feeling that their contributions are not equally valued. Either way, if such feelings are allowed to go unchecked, you have all the makings of a dysfunctional team, which will sooner or later start affecting your results. Also, if you are to live by the true spirit of brand management—that you are a guardian of the brand, running it as an entrepreneur would a business—you would not think of yourself as just the "marketing guy" in the team, but rather as a businessperson using a variety of resources (the other departments) to build your brand.

The first thing you need to recognize is that just because some contributions are not as visible as others, their value is in no way diminished. The factory worker working overtime to produce your brand, the lab technician formulating it, the lawyer ensuring that all regulatory requirements are met, the logistics manager ensuring the right product is at the right place on time—all of them play an invaluable role in enabling your brand's success, even if their efforts may not be as visible or newsworthy. The point is not that any one department plays a more important role, but that a weak link in any of them could undo all your efforts. Get to know these "unknown heroes" on your team. Recognize their contributions and jointly celebrate any success. Not only will your team pull together more, but you will become more than a marketer—you will become a leader.

LESSON 95:
Everyone screws up once in a while! Help fix the issues, don't just blame others

Many stakeholders are needed to make a brand succeed and there will always be times when something goes wrong. It could be an unexpected production issue at the factory, trucks breaking down so stocks do not reach distribution centers on time, or your sales team not getting the distribution they had planned as fast as you had hoped. It is one thing to deal with failure when it is directly in your control, such as your advertising not working or consumers rejecting a new idea for your brand. However, it is much more difficult when your brand's results are adversely affected by factors outside your immediate control, such as lapses in other departments.

When this happens, it is convenient and very tempting to pass judgment. But just remember that old saying about when you point one finger, there are four fingers pointing back. For every occasion when you think some other department has put a spanner in the works and undone all your efforts, there will be another when marketing failed to deliver on its commitments. The point is simple—nobody is infallible, and sometimes sheer bad luck can undo everything. I am not saying you should just take slip-ups lying down, but rather than griping about it, try to solve it. Elevate issues to the Decision Makers if necessary so they can help bust barriers, ask how you can help and treat setbacks as you would success—something that affects the entire team, not just one department. The true test of any team is not how it celebrates success, but in how it deals with setbacks. As a marketer, you can play a leading role in setting the tone on your brand, and in doing so, you will lay the foundations of a strong team that will rally around to help your brand succeed.

Snafu:
What to do
when things go
terribly wrong

Imagine you are crawling along a beach littered with the bodies of fallen comrades and the burning hulks of destroyed equipment. Enemy bullets are whizzing past your ears, and the worst thing is not that you are caught in this nightmare, but that you will continue to be stuck in it for the foreseeable future. If at that moment, your radio crackled to life with officers asking from the comfort of their command center on a faraway ship how things were going, how would you react? I would be tempted to ask the jerks to come and join me and find out for themselves. Thousands of US soldiers during the Second World War faced a similar situation, and dealt with it in a way that created a new addition to the English language. They would respond with the baffling term "SNAFU," which when decoded read, "Situation Normal, All F***** Up." If you want to step into the realm of real-world marketing, I would suggest that you keep yourself mentally prepared for several such situations. There will be times when you get it just right, and your brand, along with your career, take off. However, unless you are smarter or luckier than everyone I have ever known, you will screw up at times, and learning how to deal with such situations is something every marketer needs to know.

LESSON 96:
Call a spade a spade—When things look ugly, total candor is your best friend

Marketers have an unfortunate reputation of always putting a "spin" on the truth to make their products look much better than they really are. I do not believe marketers are any more or less honest than any other group of people, but this perception does have its basis in some fact. Marketers learn from training and experience that perception is reality, and the best marketers develop such a strong understanding of their consumers that they instinctively know what claims or positioning would make their brand stand apart from others, even if the basic product or service is similar, if not identical. When things go belly up, forget all you learned about managing perceptions and lay out the reality, no matter how ugly it is. Too often marketers do not confront bad news early enough and try to position it in a more positive light. Some examples:

Marketing Speak:
Our ad testing results are back, and if just one more consumer had picked us, we would have a winner.

Plain English:
The ad does not work yet.

Marketing Speak:
We may have a slight value issue versus the competition.

Plain English:
We are overpriced.

Marketing Speak:
We did well considering how tough the competitive environment is.

Plain English:
Competition kicked our butt.

While "positioning" bad news may save you from being chewed out by your bosses, it is a suicidal strategy. Not only do you risk losing all credibility when everyone realizes just how bad things are, but you also risk damaging your brand. If there are serious issues you need to tackle, you cannot wish them away, and sooner or later, they will blow up in your face.

No matter how bad things are, letting people know the unembellished truth at least makes sure they are not surprised by it later. By then it may be too late, and they may well decide that they need someone else to fix the mess! Also, having eliminated the tension of not wanting others to know how bad things are, you can focus on fixing it. I believe most marketing problems can be solved if you just ask the right questions and tackle the right issues. But most marketers are unable or unwilling to confront the real issue. If your managers are not tyrants, they will know that success and failure are both to be expected, and would much rather have a marketer on their team who identifies problems and fixes them versus someone who tries to wish them away.

LESSON 91:
One bad ad doesn't kill a brand or a career—Remember, you have equity too!

The reason why a lot of marketers are unwilling to confront failure is perfectly understandable—it is their desire to avoid being fired! While self-preservation is a fine instinct, marketing careers, like brands, tend to be much more enduring than we think. Some of the biggest brands today have faced total fiascos in the past, but emerged stronger as a result. A great example is Coke, which despite the disaster that was New Coke, rebounded and today is still an iconic global brand. Brands, like people, have reputations, and if you have done a good job of building them over time, those loyal to you will not abandon you just because you screwed up once. To take that analogy further, assume you got drunk at a party and made a fool of yourself. Would your spouse leave you because of that one incident? Unless your relationship has several other issues, I am guessing not. There will be some tension in the short term, but you should be able to get over it.

It's the same with marketers—your bosses will not dump you because of one failure. They themselves are not infallible, and I am sure they have had their share of screw-ups in their careers. Chances are when you let them know that something is seriously wrong and that you want to fix it, they will jump in and try to help out. In such a situation, it is always better to have your bosses as a part of the solution, not the problem. In fact, when you are in a tough spot, you should cast your net wide in terms of getting help; your agency could be another fabulous resource, even if your problem has nothing to do with advertising. So instead of hunkering down and trying to deal with it alone, which is often a natural tendency, shout for help—if you do not ask, you will never get it.

LESSON 98:
What doesn't kill you makes you stronger—Absorb and share lessons

Setbacks during a career in marketing come in many forms: a competitive onslaught that catches you off-guard, an advertising campaign that fails, or a new launch that never really takes off. I have experienced all these and more over the course of my career, and if there is anything more certain than the occasional setback, it is the fact that you will not be the first or last marketer to encounter it. There is nothing wrong with failing once in a while, but if you want to come out stronger from such an experience, you will need to go beyond just putting out the immediate fire.

The first thing to do once you have put the failure behind you is to step back and document what you have learned. Keep it simple—lay out what happened, what you may have missed that caused the crisis, and what steps were taken to get your brand back on track. Keep it handy for yourself and your team, and the next time you encounter a similar situation, you will not be scrambling to deal with it or relying on imperfect memories. Part of your motivation for doing this may be altruistic, in terms of helping your team, but part of it should be pure self-preservation. Everybody will understand it if you failed once, but repeatedly stumbling under similar circumstances could be a career-limiting move.

You could go one step further and share these lessons throughout your organization, so others could benefit from your experience. Chances are that others have also faced the same or similar competitors or in-market failures, and what you learned could help them out. Altruism aside, this is something that could really help you. In Lesson 84 we talked about how each marketer also needs a unique selling proposition (USP), and the depth of learning you get from such an experience (e.g. in-depth understanding of how a competitor operates) could be a valuable addition to your repertoire of skills as a marketer.

Healer, heal thyself! Some parting thoughts for the marketer

Our journey together is almost at an end, and three lessons later, this book will likely be consigned to some corner of your bookshelf or be sent back to the library where you borrowed it. I cannot presume to have covered every single topic that may interest you as a marketer or a student of marketing, but I hope to have given you some insights into real-world marketing. As a writer, most of all, I hope that I have kept you engaged and left you with a few thoughts that stay with you long after you set this book aside. In this last chapter, I do not really have any more concepts of marketing to cover, but perhaps I have something much more important to share with you. Your success as a marketer will depend on many things—your understanding of the fundamentals, your street-smarts on how to apply them in real life, and your ability to work with diverse stakeholders and resources. However, above all these lies the true secret to a long and successful career in marketing: keeping yourself energized and motivated to perform at your best. I wish I were a "life coach," in which case I would have a long lecture ready with lots of new paradigms on how to think about this and probably charge you lots of money for my advice. Unfortunately, I am and have always been a "grunt" in the battlefield of marketing—jargon bores me and fancy models put me to sleep. I believe there is no substitute for first-hand experience, expressed through plain English, so I will just share a few tips that have kept me going over my years as a marketer. Perhaps some may work for you. If you have any others that you have found useful, let me know.

LESSON 99:
Get a life and you will excel at work—My take on work-life balance

Work-life balance, or more accurately, the lack of it, is not something peculiar to marketing. It seems to be a malaise that cuts across organizations and functions, leaving stressed-out, out-of-shape executives with dysfunctional personal lives. Okay, maybe I am exaggerating a bit, but you get the point. When it comes to marketers, I believe this problem manifests itself in a couple of ways unlike many other professions. First, work-related stress for marketers is something that does not typically ebb and flow or show much seasonality—for most marketers, it is a constant. While that does offer the benefit of not having to deal with crazy swings in work demands, it also means a constant flow of pressure, a bit at a time, somewhat like Chinese water torture. Second, when you create something—a brand, a campaign, an ad or a new launch—you invest something of yourself in it. It ceases to be a purely detached business activity—to many marketers, it is very personal. That makes the perceived cost of failure and the pressure to succeed that much higher. It is impossible to advocate any one solution, because this balance is a very individual thing. However, here are some thoughts that have worked for me, which may help you as a marketer:

1. If marketing is part perspiration and a lot of inspiration, where do you get your inspiration from? In the very first lesson, we talked about success in marketing being only partly due to long hours spent toiling in front of the computer or reading research reports. To a large extent, marketing breakthroughs come when you can combine this knowledge with a spark of inspiration—a new idea, a new way of connecting consumer needs with what you offer, or a new way of going to market. I believe that the more diverse your interests, the more you open yourself up to potential new sources of inspiration. Reading a new book, playing a musical instrument, writing, just hanging out with friends—whatever works for you—I believe it is critical to have a passion outside of work. Not only does it provide a relief from work-

related stress, but engaging your mind in other activities increases the chances that you will get some new ideas or inspiration, rather than staring at your computer screen for one more hour.

2. The concept of cascading choices (Lesson 45) is not just something relevant to marketing spending choices. I have found it a useful tool to keep my work-life balance. Work is stressful, and it can consume as much of your energy as you are willing to devote to it. I always remind myself that it is just one of the roles I play in life—I am not just a marketer, but am also a husband, a son and a writer, and when I put down my cascading choices among these, there are many things above my role as a marketer. So if there is ever a conflict between staying late at the office to catch up on workplace gossip and being there for my family, the choice is a no-brainer. Like any application of cascading choices, you need to be willing to make trade-offs. Understanding the various roles you play in life keeps you grounded in the reality that your job is not the only thing in your life.

3. As marketers, we are good at setting goals for our brands, and a clear goal ensures that everything we do build it up. It is equally important, but much more difficult, to have such clarity as to what one wants out of life. There are countless tips on how to go about determining this (e.g. list 100 things you want to do before you die; close your eyes and visualize what your ideal day 10 years hence would be, etc). One thing they all have in common is that they remind us that work is important, but not the only thing in our lives. Above all, they are a means to ensure that we can do these other, more important things we want to with our lives.

LESSON 100:
What stories will they be telling about you? Leave a legacy, not assignment histories

External validation is a powerful motivator. Indeed, for most of our lives, we are conditioned to gauge our success through acceptance or validation by others—the grades we are given by others, acceptance into the "right" educational institutions, and getting a job in the company we desire. The early years as a marketer are no different: success lies in meeting the targets your boss or the company has set, and in seeing your success externally validated through salary hikes, increases in responsibility or promotions. After a time, and it may come at different points for different people, you do start wondering what you are doing with your life. It no longer feels enough to meet targets that others have set, and coming to the office every morning seems to require more motivation than congratulatory emails from the boss on some new launch. If you find yourself in such a situation, here is a way to think about it and reframe your situation.

Much of human history has relied on storytelling. Long before a single word was put down in writing, people were recording histories, spinning yarns and expanding their knowledge, all through word of mouth. Most of our epics or religious texts were oral traditions for centuries before they were written down. Modern corporate life is no different. Your sales figures may be there as testimony to how you drove a business forward, but above all, you will be remembered by the stories people will tell about you—stories your agency counterparts share with each other, stories your bosses and subordinates will share, stories that will endure after you leave your brand. Nobody will likely remember every piece of advertising you worked on or details of every quarterly sales forecast. People remember the broad strokes, and therein lies the secret to what you could use as a powerful self-motivator. People remember those who made a difference, those who broke the mold; nobody tells stories about those who just occupied their positions and did not screw up. When I step into any new assignment, I ask myself two simple questions. First, when I walk out of this assignment, how will I leave the team better than when I found it? Second, what will my legacy on the business be?

The first question concerns the legacy you want to leave for the team. If you have subordinates, it could be seeing them succeed in their careers; it could be about fixing a broken relationship with some business partners or agencies; or it could be about simplifying work processes. Whatever it is, the chance to make a real impact on someone's life is much more motivating than just peddling whatever product or service you have to. In addition, people will more likely tell stories about those who positively impacted them.

The second question concerns your legacy on the business. I am a sucker for glory (as Keanu Reeves' character said in The Replacements, "Wounds heal, chicks dig scars, but glory is forever"), so when I step into any assignment, I seek out the toughest task that needs doing—fixing a declining business and turning it around, taking on a seemingly invincible competitor, or redefining the business model. Whatever it is, I frame that big, seemingly unachievable task as my legacy and work toward it. Along the way, the usual sales targets will likely be met, and you may or may not reach this distant goal, but you would have gone for glory, not just plodded along to meet goals someone else has set. That is usually the difference between dragging yourself to work every morning to do the mundane necessities of a job and believing that you are actually doing something worthwhile—creating a legacy that will endure long after you leave the brand.

LESSON 101:
You can't be a saint, but you can do your part—Genuinely try to improve consumer lives, and equities and sales will follow

Something that never ceases to amaze me is when highly educated and well-paid marketers react to their role in society with a shrug of the shoulder and a comment like "I'm just selling _____, not creating a cure for cancer." True, most of us do not get an opportunity to do something that dramatically improves the world around us, but such an attitude just stinks of abdication of any responsibility beyond one's own narrow world of work. If you are reading this book, then either by virtue of your education or your profession, you are likely more privileged than a lot of people around you. That, in my book, is enough reason to give back something. I am not suggesting you jump into social service—that is a matter of personal choice and priorities—but there are some things you could do as a marketer. The great part is that not only do these help you do your bit to improve the lives of people around you, even if in a small way, they also make for smart business choices for your business.

I believe every marketer should be, above all, a passionate advocate of doing what is right for the consumer. Yes, there will be cost pressures, there will be swings in the way management thinks, and there will be intra-office politics. But if any of these come in the way of truly providing the best value to your consumer, you as a marketer should be the voice of the consumer within your organization who tries to prevent this from happening. It is tempting to cut back on some features that the consumer really values to save costs, or to dilute a "little bit" of performance, or to keep selling a product that may have just "minor defects that nobody will notice" to avoid the costs of a recall, or to take price increases without doing anything to enhance the consumer experience. In the short term, doing these things may even seem to make business sense. But in the longer term, such decisions inevitably have a way of catching up to you. You may not win every battle, but stand up for what is right for your consumer, and in the end you will be rewarded with sales and equities. Moreover, it is the right thing to do, and that counts more for success as a marketer than anything else you may have learned in all the preceding lessons.

When it comes time for you to take your blows in the sparring ring of marketing, and believe me you will take a few, I hope you fare better than I did in my first bout of karate. This book cannot make those blows less painful, but it can show you where they might come from and how you could deal with them. The rest, as they say, is up to you.

THE 101 LESSONS SUMMARIZED

POSITIONING

Building a better mousetrap
Creating new ideas and concepts

Lesson 1. Mix 50% inspiration and 50% perspiration—Ideation is a science and an art

Lesson 2. I know they want it, but who else offers it? Differentiate, don't imitate

Lesson 3. Remember that everyone wants free ice cream! Learn to be selective

Breaching the defenses
Sourcing share from an existing market player

Lesson 4. Aim small, hit hard—Attack on a narrow front

Lesson 5. Judo not sumo: Use competitive strengths against them

Lesson 6. Make an offer they can't refuse— Understand and break down their barriers

Enemy at the gates
Defending against competitive attack
> Lesson 7. Know who blinks first—Understand the broader strategic stakes
>
> Lesson 8. Play to the home crowd—Protect your loyal users first
>
> Lesson 9. Raise the stakes—Make the cost of victory too much to bear

There are no limits to growth
Growing a high market share brand
> Lesson 10. Would you like fries with that? Use the magic of driving consumption
>
> Lesson 11. Start a retrial factory—Continually seek new users
>
> Lesson 12. Seek new horizons—Reframe and refresh the competitive set

Empire-building
The mega-branding challenge
> Lesson 13. Create value, not just volume—Seek competency and equity fit, not just added sales
>
> Lesson 14. Would you play football without shoes? Learn the rules of the game in each category
>
> Lesson 15. Create a recurring deposit—Pay back into parent brand equity

Miracles do happen
Turning around a declining brand
> Lesson 16. Shaken and stirred—Call out a crisis, it's not business as usual!
>
> Lesson 17. Look at the bright side—what do you have to lose anyway? Think big, not incrementally
>
> Lesson 18. Remember the other "P" of marketing: Patience!

A *brand new you*
Reinventing and relaunching an existing brand
Lesson 19. When familiarity does not breed contempt—Learn the importance of keeping loyal users
Lesson 20. Substance over style—Offer something that really enhances the consumer experience, not cosmetic changes
Lesson 21. It takes more than one meeting to build a reputation—Don't move away too fast from a relaunch message

When two's a crowd
Managing a portfolio of brands
Lesson 22. No stepping on each other's toes—Pull brands apart in the consumer's mind
Lesson 23. I love you both, but… Be ruthless on the role each brand plays in your portfolio
Lesson 24. The wonder of scale—Use the portfolio to your advantage

PROMOTION
What starts well ends well
The importance of a good brief
Lesson 25. The power of one—Learn to be single-minded
Lesson 26. Good things come to those who wait—Be patient
Lesson 27. Who is going along on the journey? Be clear on who is part of the process

What if you were dating your viewer?
How to develop great TV advertising
Lesson 28. Appearances count! Learn the power of visualization
Lesson 29. Nobody dates a bore—Engage, don't ramble on about yourself
Lesson 30. The power of "ummm"—Empathize with strong insights

TAKE THE BRAND MANAGEMENT 101 QUIZ!

You've read the book, but are you really ready to take on the real world of marketing? Take this simple quiz and find out for yourself.

1. **What can marketers learn from a gentleman called Vilfredo Pareto?**
   a) Identify the few ideas that are likely to make up the bulk of your growth and focus your energy and resources on them.
   b) Be careful if you're planning to marry a penniless immigrant—she may just run away one day.
   c) The systematic application of econometric tools and principles.

2. **Your competition just introduced a costly new product feature. What could you do?**
   a) Use your existing knowledge and data on your consumer and market to quickly see if it makes sense from a consumer point of view. If it doesn't, ignore it; if it does, see what you could do to counter it fast so you don't lose out in the marketplace.

b) Hope that they're wasting their money.

c) Do detailed evaluation including large-scale quantitative research and wait for the full data to come in before you commit yourself to a point of view.

3. **What comes first in small stores in developing markets—distribution or consumer demand?**

a) A little bit of both, though to be safe, start demand creation efforts very early—together with, if not before, any distribution effort.

b) What comes first—the chicken or the egg?

c) You would need more robust multiple regression data to really establish a causal relationship.

4. **Which of these could you consider in extending a brand across multiple categories?**

a) Equity fit, the potential to pay back into parent brand equity and your knowledge of what it takes to win in the new category.

b) How much added sales will it bring? That's what matters at the end of the day, right?

c) There must be a good model somewhere for looking at such questions; you'd find that first.

5. **Which of these would classify as an appropriate use of the concept of Cascading Choices?**

a) Listing your spending choices by importance and ensuring you're spending on the most important ones before spending on the others.

b) Prioritizing getting a cold beer vs. doing this silly quiz.

c) Using quantitative models to estimate the return on investment of alternative media vehicles and then using optimization software to generate an optimum mix.

6. **What could you learn from the myth of Icarus in approaching pricing decisions?**

a) Know how high you can go without getting burnt by crossing a critical price cliff.

b) Next time you want to fly, buy an airline ticket.

c) The importance of getting accurate data before taking any decision. Icarus should never have set out without properly simulating his flight path.

7. **Your agency just presented an idea you don't think would work. How could you react?**
   a) Say that you can't buy it in its current form and explain just why it doesn't meet your specific business needs.
   b) Say tough luck and offer to buy beer in the evening.
   c) Lay out a full analysis of all the positives and negatives referencing existing consumer and market data, and identify further research that may be needed to reach a conclusive decision.

8. **What do residents of ancient Pompeii and marketers sometimes have in common?**
   a) They try and wish away potential bad news till it blows up in their faces.
   b) They drink too much.
   c) They could do with more accurate forecasting models.

9. **Why is developing TV advertising like dating?**
   a) It's all about the importance of making a strong visual impression, having empathy and not being boring.
   b) Everyone claims to do it well, but only a few are any good at it.
   c) Both are about inducing the right mix of rational and emotional responses among a desired target audience.

10. **When is launching a new item not necessarily a good idea?**
    a) When it means adding more items than you can support through marketing or in stores, or when it comes at the expense of cannibalizing your current items.
    b) When it means too much work.
    c) It's hard to say in the absence of some robust pre-market qualification that measures the potential of the new idea to build your business.

Scoring:

Give yourself 10 points every time you answered (a), 5 points for (b) and 1 point for each (c). Add up your scores and use the key below to see how you did.

Your score: _____

70-100 points means that you're ready to take the world of real-life marketing by storm!

40-70 points indicates that you probably need a refresher in some of the lessons, but at least you know the importance of being street-smart in addition to having theoretical knowledge.

0-40 points means that you probably studied pretty hard in college! Theoretical knowledge is an invaluable asset, and never lose it, but do complement it with some of the lessons in *Brand Management 101* to win in the real world of marketing.

BRAND MANAGEMENT "1 ON 1"

You've read *Brand Management 101*, but here's your chance to get "1 on 1" with Mainak Dhar. Write in with your questions on marketing and branding issues, and receive a personalized response from him. Whether it's a tough marketing issue you are dealing with at work, a concept you'd like to know more about, or just a question on some of the lessons in this book, help is just an e-mail away with "Brand Management 1 on 1"!

It's quite simple. Just write in to mainakdhar@yahoo.com.sg with the following details:

a) Your name
b) Where you live
c) What you do
d) Your question

INDEX